For Vision

For Life

For Rest

Letters to the Thirsty

70 DEVOTIONS

Edward Miller

WATERBROOK
PRESS

COLORADO SPRINGS

LETTERS TO THE THIRSTY
PUBLISHED BY WATERBROOK PRESS
5446 North Academy Boulevard, Suite 200
Colorado Springs, Colorado 80918
A division of Bantam Doubleday Dell Publishing Group, Inc.

Scripture quotations are primarily from the *New American Standard Bible* (NASB),
copyright The Lockman Foundation, 1960, 1962, 1963, 1968, 1971, 1973, 1975,
1977, and also include the author's adaptations from this version.

ISBN 1-57856-047-0

Copyright © 1998 by Edward P. Miller

Published in association with the literary agency of Alive Communications, Inc.
1465 Kelly Johnson Blvd., Suite 320; Colorado Springs, Colorado 80920

Printed in the United States of America
1998—First Edition

10 9 8 7 6 5 4 3 2 1

In memory of Gustav Rinas,
Grandpa,
a true Eleazar,
Mighty Man of King Jesus,
who clung to the sword
to his 106th year,
leaving behind the secrets
of the Lord's victory
and the spoils of the enemy

Contents

Foreword—"Always at Rest"

"I think you'll enjoy this," said my friend as he handed me a sort of homemade, computer-printed little book. I thought it looked a little corny. Assuming it would be like the dozens of not-so-great collections I get in the mail, I put it aside for several weeks.

Then one day I decided I'd better glance through it in case my friend asked me later what I thought of it. I poured a cup of coffee and settled in a rocker on our front porch. I certainly didn't expect what I found between those "homemade" covers, nor did I anticipate what would happen to my spiritual journey as a result of this first contact with the writings and insights of Ed Miller.

Now, more than five years later, thanks not only to that book but also to the "homemade" tapes of Ed and Lillian's home Bible study, I've found my horizons broadened, my understanding deepened, and my focus on an eternal perspective sharpened. Along with other "thirsty hearts" who meet at seven in the morning every Monday, I've learned through Ed's ministry to recognize the love of the Master in every book and chapter of the Bible and to cherish God's Word more passionately than ever before in my life.

Best of all, Ed has taught us all to "go for the gold" in every passage and not to get so tripped up on the words that we miss the Living Word—Christ Himself—who longs to reveal His heart to every honest seeker.

And what of Ed and Lillian Miller themselves? They have turned out to be humble, amazing people who have chosen a simple lifestyle and a straight pathway in pursuit of the One who said, "Come to Me, all who are weary and heavy-laden, and I will give you rest."

If you were to ask Ed, "What is the mark of a true believer?" his answer might surprise you. I can almost hear him say it now: "God's children are always at rest." In my hectic and stress-filled world, that is good news indeed!

Gloria Gaither

We Begin: Back to the Wonder and Joy

Dear Thirsty One,

Your suggestion is a good one, and I gladly go along with it: that we begin corresponding regularly about our spiritual growth— "the things that really matter," as you put it.

And in the pleasure of our already deepening friendship and mutual encouragement, I'm honored by your request that I begin by giving you a further glimpse into my spiritual past.

Forty years ago, when I first came to know the Savior, it was so easy. I cried out to know the Lord, He graciously revealed Himself to me, and I was gloriously changed. Here was my introduction into the truth of 2 Corinthians 3:18—

But we all, with unveiled face beholding as in a mirror the glory of the Lord, are being transformed into the same image from glory to glory, just as from the Lord, the Spirit.

Over the next seven years, however, I strayed from that foundation. It took me that long to truly embrace again the *wonder* of those core truths—that the Spirit of the Lord removes the veil from our hearts, that we behold the Lord's glory, and that we're transformed into His image from one degree of glory to another.

How and why did I wander?

First I must express my conviction that God never intended our Christian life to be complicated. When He designed our walk in Christ, He patterned it after our spiritual birth. What is miraculously true when we're born again is true also in the miracle of our daily life in Him: He reveals Himself, He does it all by His grace, and He transforms us by the revelation of the Lord Jesus.

Next I confess that at times I was like Demas, drawn away by the attraction of this world with its anxieties and riches, and devoured by its vanity. At other times I was running well, like Elijah, when suddenly a Jezebel rose up to threaten me and I was driven backward through a terrible wilderness to some dark cave in Sinai's hill. With shame I recall painful and frustrating times when I thought God owed me a blessing as a wage for my self-righteous good works. I also remember occasions when I deliberately chose darkness rather than light. In rebellion I left my first love.

Those were willful and lamentable departures from the Lord. But they were temporary, and there's something else I want to speak to you about, something deeper and more subtle in its danger.

It was when my heart longed for nothing but the living God that I truly lost my moorings. I was an earnest seeker. I had a deep and terrible yearning to know Him and abide in His presence. I dreaded separation from Him and ardently desired to find my rest in union with Him. But in my press for intimacy with Him I attempted to satisfy my hunger by that which was not bread, and to quench my thirst at broken cisterns that could not hold water.

In my desperate attempt to find the Lord, I actually looked away from Him.

I ran after good things—even spiritual things. I sought fulfillment in sound doctrine, in the will of God, in spiritual gifts, in full-time ministry. With aching heart I chased after power and victory and rest. For a season I even fell in love with the attributes of God. I worshiped the love of God rather than the God whose love it was. My heart was set on substitutes and supplements rather than on the Lord Himself.

So it was that I turned away from His grace. I became the giver rather than the receiver. I attempted to assist God in fulfilling His purposes in my life. I viewed much of His work as conditional, and therefore reasoned that all the responsibility for living in union with Him fell to me. I struggled to become His faithful and dedicated servant. I strove to be loyal and zealous to do His will.

And I became very empty. I longed for fruit in my experience, but all was barren.

To compensate, I endeavored to imitate what I perceived the Christian life to be. I became an actor. I learned the script and played the role. I went through the mechanics and the motions of enjoying the Lord. The pretense soon became obvious to those who knew me.

Then came the day—I praise God for it—when a dear Christian brother gently reached his loving hand into my broken and confused life and brought me back to the wonder and joy of my salvation in Christ Jesus. He told me the same things I had heard seven years earlier: "You need the revelation of the Lord; you need the grace of God; you need to be transformed."

How simple!

I now looked away from all but Jesus and called upon the name of the Lord. In that moment I rediscovered His first blessing and entered again into His rest.

What I had done when I first met the Savior, then repeated seven years later, I have also been doing from that day to the present. I have set my heart to know *the Lord*—not His plan, or some creedal statement about Him, or even the many mercies that flow freely from His hand. Himself I now desire, and nothing else.

The burden has been lifted. The awful bondage of playacting is behind me. I'm living in the glory of the Lord, and knowing Him is transforming my life. I trust the Holy Spirit to continue opening the Scriptures and progressively unveiling the Lord Jesus to my heart.

And I long to be one of the loving hands that reaches down to others who might have become sidetracked from the simplicity that is in Christ Jesus. I believe it would be a crime against God's mercy in my life if I did not encourage thirsty souls to return to the Lord Himself, the Fountain of living waters.

Beyond a doubt there is a generation of those who seek only His face, who earnestly desire to live in His presence and experience His fullness, and who refuse to settle for unreality. You, my friend, are one of these. You are a panter after the living God, and I'll always be grateful and privileged to pass along to you a seasonable word from the Lord, for I write as one who is eternally thankful for another brother's loving counsel that turned me again toward the Lord and His amazing grace and the manifestation of His life.

Together we're learning this:

Thirst is the coin of God's Kingdom;
Thirst is the key to supply.
"Ho! Everyone who is thirsty,
Come to the waters and buy."
Pray for a longing to know Him;
Hunger He will not deny.
Thirst is the coin of God's Kingdom;
Thirst is the key to supply.

My earnest prayer is that the Water Himself will use whatever I write to search out and satisfy your thirsty soul, and that you'll rise up to walk in Christ in the same way you received Him as Lord. I trust that all I share with you in our letters will further ground you upon the great foundations: We must know God by the revelation of the Lord Jesus through the Scriptures; we must trust His grace to provide the revelation we need; and we must allow Him to transform our lives by all that He reveals.

I eagerly await your next letter and whatever questions and thoughts it brings.

In union with Jesus,
Your brother in Christ

Letters
of Vision

1 | *He Knows That You Love Him*

Dear Tender Heart,

I know you've received many comforting words from the saints who rejoice in your restoration. They reap a harvest of gladness they have prayerfully sown in tears during your long wandering. I'm sure their consolations have encouraged you and have confirmed their love toward you.

I want to show you something that unspeakably refreshes the restored heart. It's from the Lord Himself and is found in the record of Peter's restoration in John 21.

The Lord Jesus on this occasion told Peter that he would die a martyr's death. But this prophecy was not, as might appear on the surface, a message of gloom. On the contrary it was glorious news.

After his embarrassing denials, Peter could not tell Jesus that he loved Him so much that he would be willing to die for Him. But now it was as if Jesus told him, "You fear that you'll deny Me again in the future, so let Me say for you, Peter, what you cannot say for yourself, but long to. You will not deny Me again, Peter! I will keep you. You love Me now and you'll love Me to the end, when you will prove that love by earning the martyr's crown."

I write this because I needed this word in my own restoration. It's amazing how careful we are not to boast of our loyalty after we've fallen. The law of silence, like the coal from the altar of God, burns upon our cleansed lips. The more God's light shines upon our remaining corruption, the more difficult we find it to confess love and loyalty. Our hearts become timid; memories of past offenses haunt us; and the awful possibility of breaking devotion in the future looms in our imagination. I believe we all stand with the apostle Peter at some point and are challenged to declare our love again to the Lord Jesus Christ. Often, like the prophet Ezekiel's experience, our tongue sticks to the roof of our mouth.

But the Lord knows all things. He knows that you love Him.

My dear friend in Christ, receive this word of comfort from the Lord. I know you fear the hypocrite's confession—I fear it too—but Jesus dares to say what He has worked in your heart. Jesus speaks for you. He announces your love for Him.

In the time of the Old Covenant, the worshiper always let the priest act for him. The priest offered the lamb, the priest spoke for the sinner. But now we who live in the reality and not the shadow have a glorified High Priest to act and speak in our behalf. He knows how much we love Him, and He has received His own testimony.

I pray this word will encourage you and that the confession of Jesus concerning your love will break whatever fetters your heart.

In union with the Shepherd who restores the soul . . .

2 | *He Is Yours All Along*

Dear Freed One in Christ,

I cannot fully express my joy at the news that you've set your heart afresh to spend the rest of your days knowing the Lord Jesus Christ. It's for this that we were both created and redeemed. Our full-time occupation should be knowing Him.

You must be feeling the same relief and joy that the ancient people of God felt in the year of Jubilee. Jubilee was God's wonderful provision to recover for His people the inheritance He had given to them in the first place. God originally apportioned an inheritance to each tribe. He intended that they would forever live in the bounty of it. But through the years—by neglect or necessity, by foolishness or greed—many of his people allowed the precious inheritance to slip away. Some of it was sold, some given to release a debt, some squandered. Little by little, one tribe or family forfeited or replaced the inheritance allotted to another tribe or family.

Yet how faithful God was! He established the year of Jubilee so that everyone's original inheritance would be restored.

I, too, have experienced such a Jubilee in my heart. Strange that I should ever let my inheritance in Jesus slip away—but I did. I looked with envy on other believers and foolishly traded my inheritance for theirs. Their land appeared so much more appealing than my own, and I thought that by possessing their portion I would be fulfilled. But God placed in my heart a longing for what He had given me originally. I began to ache for the Lord as I had known Him in days past. Then—oh, glorious day!—He recovered the Lord Jesus for me.

The Day of Atonement that announced the Jubilee was a day of liberty for the people of God. What a glad sound it must have been for the remnant when the ram's horn announced the breaking of chains and the canceling of debts and the full return of the ancient inheritance!

I'm sure you're aware that God did not give you a new thing when you recently determined to seek His face. No, He recovered the Lord Jesus for you; He recovered your original inheritance. God has graciously returned to you what was yours all along.

Sad, isn't it, how we allow our portion in Christ to slip away? And for what? Only bondage, debt, and estrangement from the family of saints.

The ram's horn ever sounds the heart of God, calling His own to the Jubilee. While the uninstructed press for something new, something more, something higher than the simplicity of Jesus, let us thank God for the Jubilee. What awesome grace that restores us to the fullness of the Lord Jesus!

I greatly rejoice in your restoration. I pray His grace will keep both of us from relinquishing even a portion of our inheritance in Christ.

Yours in His awesome love . . .

3 | *God Leaves You on Earth to Know Him*

Dear Friend in Christ,

In answer to your question, "Why didn't God take me to heaven the moment I trusted Jesus? Does He have a special work for me to accomplish for Him?"—I would turn your heart to a more foundational truth. God in His mercy does not keep us alive because of some mission we have to perform, but rather because He desires to reveal Himself to us on earth in ways impossible in heaven.

The benefits earth yields outstrip heaven in many ways. Take, for example, knowing God as our Sustainer through trouble. This is our privileged experience now rather than later, after all tears have been dried by His own hand. It's here on earth that God unveils to us His priesthood and enters into our sufferings, rather than in Glory where no one suffers. Only on earth does God show Himself to us as our Fortress and Defender, for who opposes us in heaven? On earth He shows Himself as our Rock and the One who lifts up our heads.

Here, when we faint, His everlasting arms catch and support us. Here He is our Savior and Advocate and gentle Shepherd. Through the changing experiences of this life we are introduced to His hands, His eyes, His feet, His wings, and His heart.

We are not left here on earth because we have a job to do, but because we have a God to know. And because knowing Him is the purpose of our existence here, we need not frustrate ourselves trying to identify our slot of service or qualifying gifts.

Oh, dear friend, follow hard after Him! Sanctify Christ as Lord and thankfully receive everything that enters your life as preparation for beholding Him in fresh ways.

You remain on earth to know God. If your heart is set on knowing Him, all else will fall into place. As He has promised, all things are working together for the good of conforming us to Jesus. Every experience in our lives is necessary preparation for the revelation of the Lord. God will reveal Himself when we are ready. He waits only for our ability to receive the truth. That is why you are not in heaven this very moment.

Do not get caught up in an activity that promises spiritual fulfillment. Do not be deceived. Far more than any job to do, far more than any work to accomplish, we have a great God to know! Doesn't this make life wonderfully simple? Let's get on with it, my friend in Christ. Let's follow on to know the Lord with all the intimacies of a marriage union.

Though this seed will not take root in every soil, your honest question deserved an honest answer, and I pray it will blossom in your heart.

God is knitting our souls together.

Your brother in Christ . . .

4 | *The Secret of True Seeking*

Dear Friend in Christ,

What a wonderful question you asked me, and what a beautiful indication of the direction of your heart! Every earnest child of God must come to understand what it means to seek the Lord.

God reveals Himself to seekers. The only measurable difference in the spiritual development between Christians is their intensity of seeking. Those who know Him the best seek Him the most.

I pray that my comments on seeking the Lord will assist you in your heart's passion to please Him. Seeking the Lord is always the heart's response to the Lord's own seeking of us.

This secret is illustrated in the record of the conversion of Zaccheus, the chief tax collector. Zaccheus will forever be known as a true seeker of Christ because he climbed into the branches of a sycamore tree for a better view of Jesus.

But at the end of Luke's record of this man's conversion, Jesus says, "For the Son of Man has come to seek and to save that which was lost" (Luke 19:10). Luke presents the Lord Jesus as the Seeker of Zaccheus, not Zaccheus as the seeker of Christ. Jesus was seeking Zaccheus, and Zaccheus simply responded to that truth.

It would not have helped Zaccheus to climb the tree if Jesus had not been coming down his street. He could have climbed a hundred trees, but if Jesus were not passing by, he would have climbed in vain. He found the Savior and His salvation because he responded to the truth that Jesus was coming down his street.

The Son of Man was seeking lost Zaccheus before lost Zaccheus began seeking the Son of Man. Zaccheus responded to His seeking, and the Lord honored that response and revealed Himself and His salvation to Zaccheus. The rich publican's life was transformed.

Jesus is always the initiator. He is the Alpha in everything— always first, and certainly the first Seeker. He is always working to get our attention. We don't always recognize His hand, but when we do, we say in effect, "Jesus is coming down my street. I think I will seek the Lord!" Seeking Jesus means responding to Jesus seeking us.

I'm thankful for your heart to seek the Lord. I will ask Him to open your eyes to the many ways and times He comes down your street. If you see Him in all events of your life, if He makes you aware that He engineers and controls all your circumstances, if you become alive to His invisible hand guiding the details of your life—then you will rise up and say, "I will seek the Lord!"

Do not try to be the first seeker. If you do, you'll be so distracted about which tree to climb that you'll wear yourself out—and in the process miss the Lord. But when you're certain the Lord is coming down your street, then climb, for Jesus cannot resist stopping at the tree of any seeker to bring salvation to his heart and home. You will seek Him when He draws you.

Never stop responding to the Lord. That is the secret of all true seeking.

Ever drawn by Him, to Him . . .

5 | *Walking with Jesus Through the Grainfields*

Dear Child of God,

I can understand your distress when some respected brothers there opposed your liberty in Jesus, suggesting that you might use your freedom to live lawlessly. Knowing your sensitive heart as I do, and knowing your passion to please the Lord in all things, I'm confident you intended no offense but were just enjoying the Lord.

I could not help but think of the day the disciples walked with the Lord Jesus in the grainfields. On that special day, a day created to symbolize our spiritual rest, they walked in union with Him and satisfied their hunger. A precious picture—walking with Jesus, walking in rest, hunger satisfied. It seems as if nothing could mar that wonderful scene.

But there were some in that day, as there are now, who lived in slavish adherence to legalism and were disturbed in the presence of those who enjoyed the Lord. They protested against the right to enjoy Jesus in such a simple way, and levied absurd and outrageous charges against both the Savior and those who walked with Him. They accused His disciples of reckless living and of willfully violating God's holy law of the Sabbath. (Some will never understand the Sabbath. The Scriptures record eight times during His ministry when people condemned our Savior for violating the day of rest, so certainly they will not hesitate to condemn the Master's servants.)

Draw comfort from remembering that Jesus Himself dealt with the Pharisees' objections that day. The disciples did not utter a word. They did not need to offer a defense. The Lord was their Defender.

The Lord has spread a table for all His children in the presence of their enemies. Walk on, dear friend, with the Lord Jesus through the grainfields of life. For the believer every day is rest; every day God satisfies our hunger; every day is fellowship with Jesus, despite the opposition of those who cannot understand.

May God Himself give you peace. Our calling is to walk with Him; He enjoys your company and delights to shepherd you along the way. He will deal with your accusers.

Relax! It's a glorious day to stroll with Jesus in the grainfields.

His friend and yours . . .

6 | *Faith in Your Friend*

Dear Friend of God,

Thank you for your most recent correspondence. I was especially moved by your closing request—"Pray that I would have the faith, surrender, and obedience of Abraham, so that if God should request from me my heart's most treasured Isaac, I would be able to lay him gladly on the altar."

Every earnest lover of the Lord Jesus has stood convicted at one time or another by the record of Abraham and Isaac on Mount Moriah. We've put ourselves in Abraham's place and wondered how we would have responded if his test were ours. Usually we come up desperately short and cry out to the Lord to continue to work patiently with us.

But Abraham had a secret. Three times the Scriptures assign a title to him that uncovers the key to his faith, surrender, and obedience: Abraham was called the friend of God. A stranger did not test Abraham; Abraham's best Friend did.

Explore with me the organic union that binds friendship to faith, surrender, and obedience.

Among strangers faith is a struggle, but not among friends. It's easy and natural to trust a friend. The closer the friendship, the more intuitive the trust. When a friend makes a request, committing our trust to him is no strain. Our unbelief would be an insult, even though we assured our friend we were doing our best to trust him. Abraham trusted God without struggle, not because his faith was great but because his friendship with God was great. Had a stranger requested the life of Isaac, Abraham would have resisted with all his strength.

What is true of faith is true also of surrender and obedience. Abraham's willingness to yield depended on his intimate union with the Lord. Since his Friend from heaven issued the command, obedience was as natural as breathing.

I underscore this relationship between Abraham's friendship with the Lord and his offering of Isaac on Mount Moriah because I take your prayer request seriously. I will pray not that God will increase your faith, but that you may cultivate a more intimate friendship with the Lord, for then faith will become automatic. I will pray not that you will be more fully surrendered, but that you'll more clearly see your true Friend. Surrender is a by-product of a relationship with God. So I will pray not that you will obey Him more fully, but that you'll know Him more deeply. God's friends keep His commandments.

I know you are earnest about this; I feel honored that you invited me to pray. If God answers my prayer, your eyes will be turned away from faith, surrender, and obedience, unto the Lord Himself. I am convinced that as you walk in union with Him you'll receive the faith, surrender, and obedience for which you long. May Abraham's secret become ours.

In Him who is no stranger . . .

7 | *Beyond Lordship Is Friendship*

Dear Bondslave of Jesus,

Jesus is Lord! What a comfortable pillow for our heads in all circumstances. And God has begun to open my heart to what can be spoken of as the consummation of His lordship.

At times in our conversations you and I have climbed high in our contemplation of His universal and personal reign as King of kings and Lord of lords. But we did not reach the highest rung.

As we've discussed, a glorious day is coming when every enemy will be subdued and put under His feet. All rule, all authority, every form of government, all resistance and opposition, and every stronghold of error, ignorance, and lawlessness will bow before Him who is Lord of all.

And we read that the last enemy to be abolished is death. All will be conquered in the final overthrow of death; nothing will remain to be subdued. Finally, all will be under His feet. We would therefore expect victory over death to be His ultimate triumph, His crowning act.

But there is more. In 1 Corinthians 15:28, the apostle Paul writes,

> *And when all things are subjected to Him, then the Son Himself also will be subjected to the One who subjected all things to Him, that God may be all in all.*

Don't be afraid to pull out all the stops and enter the thrill of what is being proclaimed here. When Jesus is finally Lord of all, He lays down everything at His Father's feet. Just as in His humility He did not grasp at equality with God, so in His exaltation He does not grasp at the prerogatives that belong to the King of kings. By submitting all to God the Father, He chooses to enter eternity as our Kinsman, our Brother, the Son of Man, One with us and not One over us. His goal is friendship, anticipated in His words in John 15 to His disciples:

> *You are My friends if you do what I command you. No longer do I call you slaves, for the slave does not know what his master is doing; but I have called you friends, for all things I have heard from My Father I have made known to you.*

Oh, dear friend in Christ, do you perceive this glorious truth? Even now He wants to be Lord only so He can become our Friend. The highest rung on the ladder of His lordship is friendship. He gloriously subdues all of our enemies, not so He can lord it over us but so He can draw near to us as our Friend. Beyond lordship is friendship; He conquers in order to be intimate with us.

I'm ashamed to think how often I resisted His lordship in my life because I did not realize He wanted intimacy with me.

He will reign until the last enemy is subdued, and when He is Lord of all He will lay down the crown and invite me into union with Himself.

Oh, may God help us to know the intimate consummation of His lordship!

I welcome your comments and insights into this thrilling truth.

Yours in His victory . . .

8 | *Grow in Christ by Letting Christ Grow in You*

Dear Growing Believer,

I hope I caused no confusion when I spoke to the saints meeting in your home about our growing in the Lord Jesus by allowing Him to grow in us. I'll try in writing to communicate more of God's heart on this and clear away any misunderstanding.

Under the inspiration of the Holy Spirit, the apostle Paul pictures our Lord Jesus as an unborn baby in the wombs of the Christians in Galatia. Paul desired that Christ be formed in them as a child is formed in its mother (Galatians 4:19). There is a glorious mixing of metaphors here. The apostle spoke of himself as the one in labor pains, but the believers were the ones carrying the baby. Paul was in labor until Christ was formed in the saints. This is the heart of the New Covenant: We labor that Christ may be formed in others. It is all part of redemptive living. Paul's great longing was not for the believers to become active in Christian service or to become generous givers or to live separated lives. Paul longed supremely that Christ be formed in believers.

Our growth in the Lord depends on His being formed in us. As our vision of Him increases, He "grows" in us. The greater our conception of Him, the more we will appropriate Him by faith.

I fear that many Christians are so occupied with their own growing in Christ they aren't beholding Him by revelation. They concentrate on growing through study, prayer, fasting, fellowship, the means of grace, ministry, missions, and a host of other activities that actually hinder spiritual growth when pursued as a goal.

The Lord desires us to grow. He longs to increase our heart's affection for Him. He delights to reveal His greatness, His fullness, His all-sufficiency. The larger He becomes, the more eager we are to live in ways that mirror His character. His growth in us is revelation. Our growth in Him is transformation. We grow by every new vision of Him.

Always there is only one rule that we must grow by: We must see Jesus!

Dear friend in Christ, like the apostle I yearn that the Savior grow in your spirit. That is my joy, my fruit—my baby. In that sense I love you with a mother's love. I have no doubt that if Christ develops in your life as a child develops in the womb, in due time He will be growing in you and you will deliver Him to the world.

May it come to pass. His growth in you is your hope of growing in Him.

Greet the saints for me.

Yours, in the heart-knowledge of the Lord . . .

9 | *God Himself Is Your Armor*

Dear Fellow Soldier of our Lord Jesus,

I know you'll soon be coming in your study of Scripture to the grand section in Ephesians about the belt of truth, the breastplate of righteousness, the sandals of the gospel of peace, the shield of faith, the helmet of salvation, and the sword of the Spirit. Perhaps a word of personal testimony will spare you the frustration I endured in investigating this passage.

I researched every piece of the Roman armor—belt and breastplate, sword and shield, everything from the helmet to the studded military sandals. I thought that if I understood each piece of armor, I could relate it to spiritual reality and apply it to my life. I intended to appropriate the Christian's armor one piece at a time. In so doing I completely missed the wonder of the armor—and almost missed the Lord!

From his prison cell the apostle Paul beheld a Roman guard in military dress and thought, *That guard in his armor is exactly like the Christian in his God.* The armor is one thing: God Himself. We are told to "put on the whole armor *of God.*" Our security does not lie in figuring out each piece of armor but in being clothed from head to foot in the Lord Himself. He is our armor and protection from the wiles of the devil.

Dear friend in Christ, do not pursue what is not Him. As I've mentioned, for many years I chased after the streams and missed the fountain. I ran after faith and righteousness and ministry and a score of other things that were not the Lord. I even sought many mercies closely connected to His person. I sometimes wonder if God is not wounded when His own beauties and attributes obstruct our clear view of Him. I want to spare you the vanity that parched my life for so many years.

Of course I am not suggesting that you forgo a thorough study of the details of the Christian armor. In fact, when you're ready, I have a treasury of material to expedite your research. Study the armor, but not as those who desire to be well-protected. Study as those who *already* are well-protected, armored in the person of the Lord Jesus Christ Himself.

The simplicity of the armor is in the taking. Could there be a greater safety than to be clothed in God?

Your fellow soldier in Christ . . .

10 | *Your Pure Spiritual Water*

Dear Peacemaker,

I'm glad to hear you've avoided the recent controversy that has brought confusion into the fellowship there, and great grief to the heart of our dear Lord Jesus.

Doesn't this make you long for the crystal river that flows from under the throne of God and from the Lamb? If God's people would press on to this virgin fountain they could be so refreshed and satisfied. But confusion and disunity come from living downstream.

The Jordan River, as it moves down to the Dead Sea, gathers sediment and impurities from countless tributaries. But somewhere thousands of feet high on Mount Hermon it has a sweet beginning, a crystal-clear source, uncontaminated by the things it will pick up later.

So often God's people aren't drinking from the river as it bubbles at its source, clean and cold and refreshing. They drink from where it has been spoiled by speculations, human wisdom, and proud systems over which God's people splinter and divide.

May God teach us to trace out the Living Water, and may He deliver us from fighting over muddy currents. Let us be ever pressing on to the throne and the Lamb. The nearer we approach Christ and His finished work, the clearer the water will flow and the more refreshing it will be.

Let us be numbered with those who have no time or taste for any water but that which flows from the throne and the Lamb. We must move onward and upward; we cannot force those who drink from muddy waters to join us, but we can invite them to accompany us into His glorious presence.

You have wisely disassociated yourself from those who drink the bitter waters of disunity. You have shown yourself a true elder by smiling and pressing on.

We have a better fountain, a crystal river, the Lord Jesus Himself! What a glorious foretaste of heaven.

Yours for the unity of believers . . .

11 | *He Loves Because He Loves*

Dear Object of His Delight,

Your insight into God's amazing mercy cheered my drooping spirit. Here's a thought on His love that I pray will encourage your own heart to sing.

Moses had a wonderful word for God's redeemed remnant as they stood near the Jordan River, ready to enter the Promised Land. His words recall the question every thinking child of God has asked at one time or another: "Why me? Why did God choose me? Why did He set His love upon me?"

Why does God love His own? Hear the profound words of the Holy Spirit through His servant Moses in Deuteronomy 7:7–8—

> *The LORD . . . set His love on you . . . because the LORD loved you.*

God loved them because He loved them—and He loves you because He loves you! He loves me because He loves me!

He loves us because He loves us. He chose us just because He chose us. If God's ancient people found peace in knowing this, that same peace can be ours as well. God loves us with an unchanging love that never had a starting point and never will come to an end. His love will endure through the ages of eternity simply because He loves us.

Oh, chosen one of God, take consolation from this mighty truth: You are the object of His love. Nothing we are, have, or do will ever increase His love toward us. He cannot love us more; He will not love us less; the spring of His love will ever be His love. There it is in all its beauty, wonder, and mystery.

Here's a way my heart sings this truth:

He loved me because He loved me;
He proved it at Calvary!
If value is made by the price that is paid,
Then His blood made a treasure of me!

Believe it! Rest in it!
May this truth bring music to your heart.

Loved into union with Jesus . . .

12 | *His Silver Cup in Our Sack*

Dear Friend in Christ,

You used the word *strange* to describe God's recent providence in your life; you also called it "mysterious and baffling." I'm delighted by your willingness to allow God to teach you during this difficult time.

Perhaps I can shed some light on the direction God seems to be moving in your life. For me, identifying a direction is more helpful than trying to comprehend some specific purpose God may have. The Bible contains the best illustration of this.

When Joseph decided to reveal himself to his brothers, he did something that appeared "strange, mysterious, and baffling." He planted a silver cup in the sack of his youngest brother, Benjamin. Why? On the surface Joseph seemed to be playing a cruel, heartless trick on his brothers, but it proved to be a turning point for them and caused them to search their hearts and repent. The silver cup accomplished what many years of trials had failed to produce.

Allow me to rehearse what led to the planting of that wonderful cup. When his brothers came down to Egypt, Joseph was a stranger to them. He loved them and longed for the day he could say, "I am Joseph!" But they were not ready for that yet. Several times Joseph stole away from their presence to weep in private because he could not tell them who he was. Joseph grieved that his brothers stood before him only because he was the only one who could fill their empty sacks.

And how much more is God grieved when our prayers amount to "take my gift; fill my sack; and dismiss me as a stranger"!

Joseph wanted more than to provide for his family. He also wanted to be no more a stranger to them. If not for the silver cup planted in the sack, they would have departed from Joseph's presence and never known him; but because of it they had to return to him and he could then reveal himself to them. By the silver cup they came to know their provider in a personal way.

God has filled my own sack with grain many times, and then I went on my way to devour it. He had blessed me even though I did not recognize Him. But I used up the grain quickly—and hunger quickly drove me back to His feet.

Then one day I found a silver cup in my sack—a severe mental suffering. Oh, I praise Him for the love that refused to send me on my way with a full sack and an empty heart. The silver cup arrested me and presented Him with the opportunity to reveal Himself.

God loves us too much to allow us to remain strangers.

The silver cup has taken many forms in the history of God's redemption: affliction, trial, loss, disappointment, terrible reversal, or hurt. Heaven will be full of testimonies of silver cups. We'll hear how the broken marriage, the bankruptcy, the blunder, the accident, the disease, the storm, the act of violence, the breakdown, the strong hand of the law, and many other precious goblets were wisely placed in the saints' full sacks to bring them to the knowledge of the Lord Himself.

I think of it this way:

In mercy He adds to the cross I must carry,
In grace every trial by Him is bestowed;
He knows in my weakness I'll run straight to Jesus;
He adds to the burden to lighten the load!

So when the Lord places the cup (whatever it is) in our sack—shall we not drink from it? I cannot say with certainty that your present situation is God's silver cup, but it may be. It *is* consistent with His great heart. He will not continually send His children away with a fullness that is not Him.

Do not fear the silver cup, my tested friend. Do not resent it. The Lord isn't playing some shabby trick on you. It is God's wonderful provision to liberate His children for the wonders of His lordship. Aren't you glad with heaven's joy that your best Friend will do whatever it takes to reveal Himself to you?

If you conclude that He has indeed planted a silver cup in your sack, thank Him for it and prepare for the revelation of Christ.

If you do not find it to be a silver cup, do not go on a silver cup hunt. He rules in such a way that the silver cup finds *us.*

In all cases, seek His face!

Yours, in His mysterious love . . .

13 | *When the Hedge Is Down*

Dear Precious Saint of the Lord,

Your faith in the midst of your trial has encouraged us who have not been so severely tested. Your continued joy in the Lord has silenced the enemy's insinuation that God is not always wonderful and worthy of worship and praise. Satan's ancient accusation against Job—that the Lord is loved and trusted only because He surrounds His children with the hedge of blessing—has been overthrown again by your patient endurance and fervent love of Jesus.

Thank you for demonstrating to the church the all-sufficiency of the Lord even when the hedge is down. You have reminded us that the Lord is wonderful not because of what He does or gives but because of who He is. Apart from all His gifts He is lovely and worthy of our trust.

Your objective faith in such a worthy Savior challenges those of us who tend to be more subjective. How refreshing it is to see you resting in His presence even when He seems absent. You can rejoice without physical evidence of Him—and that example spurs us on to embrace Him for who He is. You've turned our hearts from the gifts to the Giver.

I pray we will never dishonor the Lord by measuring His sufficiency by the many blessings He lavishes upon us. We can become so attached to our precious hedge! But you have shown us where true sufficiency lies.

Solomon said, "Wealth makes many friends." But what kind of person befriends another merely because of wealth? Our Lord Jesus doesn't need such friends. You have shown yourself a *true* friend of the Savior, and we're all richer for your suffering.

Your profoundly thankful friend . . .

14 | *Be Comfortable with Your Past*

Dear Child of His Mercy,

What a strange unbelief that would suggest the confession you penned in your sad note to me—"I think I will never feel comfortable again in the presence of the Lord. My past destroys my present."

In the presence of Jesus you can indeed feel comfortable with your past. Jesus is not cruel; He does not desire His forgiven children to labor under the weight of guilt or to feel condemned because of past failures.

Our resurrected Lord revealed this wonder to Peter on the shores of Galilee. There in John 21, Jesus wasn't trying to resurrect a memory that would make Peter squirm. By choosing to cook breakfast on a charcoal fire, Jesus was not attempting to shame Peter with the memory of the charcoal fire the night of his disloyalty. Jesus wasn't trying to intimidate Peter when He called him

Simon—his pre-salvation name—instead of Peter, "the Rock." Our Lord did not mean to embarrass Peter with a reminder of his three denials when He asked this disciple three times to confess his love afresh.

Our beloved Friend knew the bondage that comes with failure, and He knew Peter would never be free if he continued to suppress his past. Jesus did not want Peter to cringe every time someone called him Simon, or he saw a charcoal fire, or he heard a rooster crow. Jesus did not bring up Peter's past to make him uncomfortable, but to demonstrate that the past was no issue with Him.

With the past in public view, Jesus invited Peter to "Come and dine." It's as if Jesus said, "Come, My child; do not allow the past to interfere with wonderful fellowship with Me. The past is not at all in the way. We can fellowship perfectly with your past in plain view. I am comfortable with your past; you may also be comfortable with it in My presence."

Be sure, my friend in Christ, that your fellowship with our Lord Jesus is not hindered by your past. Come and dine with Him! If we feel shame, let it come because our Lord Jesus was cruelly treated because of our sin, and not because of our past—forgiven!—sin.

May He grace us to have the pastlessness of a newborn baby. May we be forever comfortable in the presence of Jesus.

Yours, by His awesome mercy . . .

15 | *The More of Him You See, the More There Is to See*

Dear Beholder of Jesus,

You raised provocative questions about the miracle Jesus performed on the blind man of Bethsaida (Mark 8). I wouldn't call the work of the Lord Jesus imperfect, just incomplete. When Jesus anointed and touched the blind man the first time and the man testified, "I see men . . . like trees, walking about," the first touch readied the man for additional touches.

I'm glad the Holy Spirit included this miracle in the gospel record so that we have this wonderful illustration of progressive revelation and illumination. We need not only the Lord's first and second touch, but also to be touched by Him again and again. The infinity of the Lord requires this.

Since Jesus is infinite, our sight of Him can never be complete. We can only begin to comprehend the infinite. There will always be more of Him concealed from us than there is revealed. Like the blind man who received his sight, we'll behold Him with an incomplete vision; we will always see in twilight. Even in eternity, when we'll pursue Him with glorified capacities, we will never overtake Him. We will never exhaust His wonder and His beauty. We will ever see Him "as trees, walking."

This has been our experience of Him since our first trusting look. When I first saw Him by faith, my eyes and mouth were opened wide in amazement. My heart cried out, "I heard He was wonderful, but I never knew He was like this!"

Time went on; my eyes and mouth opened wider with additional amazement. Now my heart still is singing, "I never dreamed He was like this!" In the days ahead I fully expect to receive His touch again, and that touch will continue to open my eyes afresh to behold new aspects of His beauty.

So shall it ever be—even in Glory. A billion billion years of additional revelation will pass and I'll be singing, "Holy! Holy! Holy! I always knew You were wonderful, but I never imagined You were like this!" At each revelation we shall look back and confess that we have seen Him but dimly.

The more of Him we see, the more of Him there is to see.

Let us press on, dear friend. We must let Him touch us, that by His good grace we will be able to walk in the light He gives until we're ready for an additional touch. His fresh touch will keep correcting our limited vision, and so we'll keep advancing in Him.

May our continual need of His touch keep us humble. His revelation graciously waits on our capacity. When we are ready, He will touch us again . . . and again . . . and again!

Yours, in the progressive vision of Him . . .

16 | *You Are His Garden*

Dear Fragrance of Christ,

In your recent letter I sensed that you're unsettled due to your desire to always please the Lord. Strange that your joy should be drained by so noble a thirst.

Perhaps God will show you the same sweet discovery the Shulammite made in the beautiful Song of Solomon. She was so in love with her groom that she set her heart to live for his pleasure. She kept a watchful eye for every little fox that threatened to spoil any vine; she attempted to make herself attractive for her groom; but she also became too sensitive to her flaws and began to cultivate a self-deprecating spirit.

The groom, on the other hand, was captivated by her beauty. She was already attractive to him, and he viewed her as his precious garden. He was not at all bothered by a single weed, but only enthralled with the glory of his cultivation. She was his garden, enclosed and sealed—the joy of his heart!

She was surprised to realize that he regarded her as his garden and not his gardener; that she existed for his pure enjoyment and not his employment. When she discovered this truth, she loved him all the more. She prayed (in 4:16):

Awake, O north wind, and come, wind of the south; make my garden breathe out fragrance, let its spices be wafted abroad. May my beloved come into his garden and eat its choice fruits!

The bride did not lose her desire to please her groom, but it was no longer a burden to her. She began to rest in what she knew delighted his heart.

Nothing else mattered. Her groom accepted her as she was, and that was enough. She was no longer afraid of the north wind, though it blew cold and brought adversity and blighting frost; nor was she partial to the south wind, though it blew pleasant and with the promise of prosperity. She courted every wind that promised to waft her fragrance to her lover.

Dear friend in Christ, with joy I remind you that you are well accepted in the Beloved. You do not need to add to your beauty and standing before Him. You are His garden and He desires to enjoy you. Many winds have already blown through your life, and every one of them has pleased your Groom.

He is pleased with *you*. You are His bride, His garden. It is you, dear friend, who makes the Groom's heart beat faster. So relax!

Resting in His love . . .

17 | *Arise and Run with Him*

Dear Fellow Seeker,

My recent meditation on the Song of Solomon brought home to my heart your caution against limiting the Lord. Like the bride in the story, I realized I had been gazing at the Lord from behind a lattice.

In Solomon's lovely song, the bridegroom comes leaping like a gazelle or a young stag over the hills and the mountains, seeking the sweet fellowship of the object of his heart. He comes calling to his dear bride, "Arise my darling, my beautiful one, and come along. . . . [L]et me see your form[,] . . . let me hear your voice." The bridegroom wants his bride to arise from her lattice view to a full and liberating vision of him.

The bride in the love song is too fearful to leave her comfortable surroundings; she would be pleased if he would join her inside the lattice hedge. But he refuses to enter her confining enclosure. He is free! Alive! Unlimited! He wants to remain free and refuses to be imprisoned. *Arise, my darling, my beautiful one, and come along*—this is his great desire. The groom wants the bride to run, leap, dance, and frolic with him in uninhibited freedom of spirit. He invites her into his wonderful world.

Lately I have been as the bride, squinting through the lattice with only a partial view of Him. The boundaries I thought would enclose Him near my heart actually barred Him from me. One moment He was visible, the next He could not be found. Even when in view, His form seemed indefinite and dark. I not only hurt myself by the legal restraints I had erected around me, but I also was denying the Groom the pleasure He sought in my company.

You'll be pleased to know I've gladly responded to the Groom's invitation to live free with Him. He is wider than the most generous frontier that man ever assigned to Him.

Oh, my friend in Christ, when the Groom calls, let us spring up quickly and gladly and discover the thrill of His boundless fellowship. Though some may count us reckless, let us not be afraid to leave behind everything that confines the Lord. We must not imprison the Groom with our narrow doctrines or limited experiences of Him. May we never attempt to draw our wonderful Savior into the restricting limits of our own understanding.

We must not be afraid to be free and run with Jesus wherever He desires to run, no matter how radical that fellowship appears. Let those who still struggle with the Old Covenant content themselves with a lattice vision of Jesus. We cannot! We must see Him in full view. We must rise at His invitation and run with Him in liberty.

Jesus is beautiful, even through the lattice. But oh, how much more beautiful He is on the other side of it! May God grace us to discard every lattice that we might behold Him in His unveiled loveliness. One sight of Jesus as He is and we will never again settle for a lattice vision.

Thank you, my friend, for the faithful nudge.

Your grateful brother . . .

18 | *Already, God Prepares Your Provision*

Dear Child of His Love,

Thank you for letting me know of your genuine need. I cannot say how the Lord will provide for it. No Christian, no matter how experienced or intimate with the Lord, can predict how God will rescue him or her. He is a God of infinite variety. He deals with each of His children according to his or her uniqueness and His purpose to uniquely conform each one to the Lord Jesus. You can rest in the fact He will provide for you in the fullness of His time and purpose.

You have not passed this way before, but I would encourage you to trust the precious Holy Spirit to keep your eyes focused—not on God's provision but on the Lord Himself. If you do, then like Abraham you will discover that God always has a ram climbing up the blind side of the mountain.

It was only after Abraham reached the altar and raised the knife over his son Isaac's heart that God intervened, and only then did Abraham look up and see the Lord's provision—a ram caught in a thicket. Had Abraham stopped short or disobeyed, he would have missed the blessing of discovering God's ram.

The side of the mountain you're called to climb may appear rough and barren with no sign of escape. Obey, by God's grace, to the end. Already God has begun to grow the thicket of thorns; already the ram is being prepared.

After your heart is tested, God will open your eyes. Then all will be clear. Thousands of His elect have found it so. Sight sees the altar, the blood, the fire, the beloved Isaac; faith sees the thorn-crowned ram and the glory of the Resurrection. Faith must embrace both death and resurrection.

Do not try to see what is on the blind side of the mountain. See only God! And in seeing Him you can rest, for the ram is on its way to your altar.

In union with Jesus . . .

19 | *See Him, Then Surrender*

Dear Friend of the Covenant,

I'm glad to explain my warning about surrender being a possible hindrance to union with the Lord Jesus Christ. My personal testimony has confirmed what I've recently found to be God's revealed truth. In my passion to be a whole burnt offering for Him, I became so focused on surrender that I almost missed the Lord.

One may become so surrender-minded that his entire life is taken up with the process of yielding. I sought to surrender not only my body but each of its members, every loved one in my family by name, the contents of our home, and even every book in my library. I begged the Lord to receive the offering of my works, my responsibilities, my ambitions, my talents, my friends. The surrender was never complete. Every Christian I met or message I heard brought on fresh condemnation by suggesting I had not made a complete commitment. The painful process of surrender would begin again.

I discovered I had totally surrendered to a very small vision of the Lord. I had seen Him as God's spotless Lamb taking away the sin of the world, but I had seen little of Him beyond that. I needed a fuller vision of God. I struggled because I was trying to surrender to Him the areas in which He was a stranger to me.

Heart surrender is assumed in the lives of those who are genuinely His. A more complete surrender is not needed; a fresh revelation of the Lord through the Word of God is. When one beholds the Lord, *then* there is something to surrender to.

I long that you, dear servant of the Lord, will quickly learn this reality. If only God's people would run more often to the Holy Spirit's feet to behold the Lord Jesus rather than to the altar, they would gain so much more. We are saved to see Him. If we truly behold Him, surrender is never a problem.

Let us press on to see Him. Let us ask God to open our eyes to His glorious person, His offices, His works, His titles, His ways, His life, His dealings with His saints, His relationships. Let us earnestly chase after Him—all that speaks of Him, foreshadows Him, exalts Him. Great and glorious is our Lord! If God would fill our eyes with Him, surrender would follow swiftly. "Show me, I pray Thee, Thy glory," prayed Moses. Let us pray it as well.

I trust this is not a mere juggling with semantics, but a direction of the heart. May the Lord enlarge our vision of Him. I reverently pray Ephesians 1:17–23 for you, which I pray you will read at your leisure.

Bound hand and foot to Jesus . . .

P.S. Find enclosed the testimony as only poetry can express it . . .

SURRENDER

On countless altars I have laid the world and all concerning me;
Unnumbered tear-stained vows were made, then broken, to my
 agony!
How to resign? Be His at last? Abandon self? I did not know!
'Twas not the world that held me fast; surrender was my greatest
 foe.

Was faith to blame? Did I not seek? What evil kept me from my
 quest?
Some secret sin? Was flesh too weak? Was Satan keeping me
 from rest?
Must I forever rise and fall? Is there no power to break the sway?
How often must I give my all and take it back the very day?

I tried in vain to give Him more; the light of hope was growing
 dim;
Surrender was the barrier that kept my homesick heart from
 Him.
Is His arm short? Will He not hear? Is He reluctant to receive?
Is He not ever drawing near to grace the sinner to believe?

I could not yield; I could not die; my spirit like the moonlight
 waned;
I wearied of the question, "Why?" and o'er my life confusion
 reigned.
For if surrender was the key to know the Lord and be made full,
Then why the struggle to be free? Why was it so impossible?

As blossoms drop ere fruit can grow, as dissipates the morning dew,
As darkness flees before the day, or breath of spring makes all things new,
My wilted root, by unseen Hand, was guided on its thirsty course,
Wending its way through barren land, to tap at last the Living Source.

One glimpse of HIM and all the strain and struggle did at once depart;
Those things I counted once as gain appeared as rubbish to my heart.
As lovers need no influence all rival loves to set aside,
I felt in His preeminence that now my heart was crucified.

Who finds the treasure counts no wealth too dear or difficult to give;
Who would not trade disease for health or give up death and choose to live?
As children gladly drop the toy their loving parents to embrace,
Surrender was my greatest joy while gazing on His lovely face.

No eagle in its lofty flight above the world could be so free;
My soul with effortless delight enjoyed the Lord with liberty.
Now HIM I seek, not how to give, deny, or mammon to forsake.
For me, to know Him is to live! Surrender follows in the wake.

Letters
of Life

20 | *God's Best Grace Is Yours*

Dear Helper in Grace,

I appreciate your intercession during this difficult time in my life. I don't doubt that I'll be sustained by God's all-sufficient grace. I do not regard my circumstances as unique, and I draw comfort from knowing that the grace that sustained the great apostle in 2 Corinthians 12 can be appropriated for my lesser thorn. God's grace for Paul is God's grace for me.

Was ever a Christian more grounded in the New Covenant than Paul? Could there be a more spiritual experience than being caught up into the third heaven and appearing in the presence of the Lord?

Likewise, could there be a more savage attack on a believer than what Paul described as "a messenger of Satan" buffeting his flesh with a "thorn"?

So it was that the best Christian, in his most spiritual moment, came under the most infernal attack, and found the grace of God to be all-sufficient for his need. Shall I find less?

All Christians are represented here by the best, all experiences by the highest, and all opposition by the worst. Therefore I'm left without any excuse if I do not appropriate the grace of God in my hour of need.

By God's overruling power, Satan's messenger was required to carry the message of God to the suffering apostle. The thorn by which Satan sought to pamper Paul's pride instead humbled him. God turned to His glory the sharpest thorn ever to penetrate a Christian's flesh.

Every thorn is allowed by God to press us to His embrace. In His glorious presence and in union with Him, we receive His liberal and adequate grace to equip us to bear the thorn redemptively.

I'm being fed with this substantial wisdom, my praying friend. I will live to praise Him for the thorn that now goads me toward the One who is my uncreated fountain of help.

We are by nature unstable pilgrims in a very slippery world. There is not a passing moment when we can say, "We have no need of His all-sufficient grace." Our Savior, who prayed for Peter's safety before Peter ever suspected his danger (Luke 22:31–32), is praying for us.

I do not expect like Paul to be caught up literally into the third heaven (before my mortal body is clothed with immortality), but I expect a foretaste of the third heaven by God's revelation of His Son to my heart. I don't expect to be as severely buffeted by Satan's messenger as Paul was, but surely the tempter will try to destroy me through a proud spirit. I don't expect to endure the same thorn Paul did, but I expect the same grace.

I am not Paul, but I serve his God. I may drink from the same fountain that slaked his thirst.

Thank you for praying for me. Let your petitions be saturated with gratitude and praise for His wonderful grace in my life. I am the lesser, and my provision is included in the greater.

And when the sky begins to clear, when clouds no longer roll,
I'll see the Lord and know the storm was under His control!

Kept by His amazing grace . . .

21 | *Spiritually Unformed and Unfinished*

Dear Handiwork of God,

Since I asked you to pray for me, it's only right that I inform you
of God's gracious answer to my heart's cry. I cannot honestly say
that I've become more spiritually mature, nor can I claim a greater
victory over the corruption in my heart. I still hate my sinful
thoughts, and I still long for the day when I shall be conformed to
the image of Christ. Sanctification is a slow process; I would be
glad to learn of a shortcut to maturity.

But this morning the Lord refreshed my spirit with Psalm
139:16. David prayed,

> *Thine eyes have seen my unformed substance; and in Thy book
> they were all written, the days that were ordained for me, when
> as yet there was not one of them.*

I've always enjoyed this passage, but I restricted it to the nine months I spent in my mother's womb. There I was conceived; there I began to be formed; there all of my needs were abundantly provided. Throughout my prenatal existence nothing was hidden from the Lord. He reviewed my future before my first day had dawned. What a picture of His amazing sufficiency and my absolute helplessness. Even then He was a Giver and I a receiver.

The new and refreshing light I received from this wonderful text is the realization that my life is still unformed. I am as helpless now as I was then—now, as then, I can do nothing except receive God's provision. Whether I'm in the womb or out, God sees my unformed substance.

Today I'm as undeveloped spiritually as I was physically when in my mother's womb. When I enter eternity, I suppose I'll be as oblivious to this world as I am now to the world of my mother's womb. When I'm like Him, I will look back and realize there was never a need for a moment's concern. His business has always been to make us like Him.

Slowly being changed . . .

22 | *Resurrection Precedes Death*

Dear Co-laborer in the Lord,

I don't hesitate to answer your recent heart cry: No, I know of no shortcut to the death of self. Yet there's a paradox in the way God accomplishes that death.

I know you long to die to self that you might live unto God. Thousands of Christians struggle with this issue because they believe they must first die before they can enjoy resurrection life. The enemy subtly deceives us into confusing the starting point with the goal.

Strange as it may sound, for the Christian experience, resurrection must precede death. Death is the fruit of resurrection. We do not die to self in order to enjoy a living Savior; we enjoy a living Savior in order to die to self!

Please consider this, my hungry friend: To give ourselves

redemptively to the Lord requires the power of His indwelling life. Beholding the Lord is always the beginning. The revelation of the Lord Jesus is the fountainhead of all faith and surrender.

It is futile to fight flesh with flesh. We cannot crucify the self. The power to die to self comes only from an intimate union with the living Lord Himself.

The apostle Paul longed to know Christ in the power of His resurrection in order to be made conformable unto His death (Philippians 3:10). Resurrection comes first.

This revelation may not provide you a shortcut to the death of self, but it will deliver you from the Christless struggle so many endure for many years. Do not attempt to die that you might live; live that you might be empowered to die.

Relate to the risen Savior and you will discover the master key to the crucified life. Go after Him with all your heart, soul, strength, and mind, and as a by-product of that union you'll find yourself supernaturally baptized into His sufferings and conformed to His death.

I'm persuaded that your real passion is the life of Christ, not the death of self. May God grace you to die by the power of His life that the world may find life in your death.

Yours, in a living Savior . . .

23 | *Your Highest Obedience*

Dear Servant of the Living God,

You aren't the first Christian to wrestle with the question of what is God's part and what is man's. (I'm thrilled that you aren't struggling with *whether* to obey God, only with *how* to obey Him.)

I was helped to answer this question by meditating on the great commission Noah received, and by observing how he obeyed it. In Genesis 7, God commanded Noah,

> *Enter the ark . . . you shall take with you of every clean animal by sevens, a male and his female; and of the animals that are not clean two, a male and his female; also of the birds of the sky, by sevens, male and female, to keep offspring alive on the face of the earth.*

At first glance it would appear that Noah's assignment was to go throughout the earth and gather representatives of every creature—animals, birds, insects. I believe these creatures also represent mankind, just as they did in Peter's vision at Joppa. God showed Peter He made no distinction between any He had cleansed, whether Jew or Gentile. Noah's great commission foreshadowed the vision in Joppa; Noah was to bring into the ark that which symbolized every part of humanity.

How did Noah obey this command? Did he run through the forests and fields with traps, nets, goads, and whips in his hands? Did he lure the creatures in by some clever ruse? Did he work alone or did his family offer assistance?

The record is wonderful, my dear friend in Christ, and full of humbling truth. Before Noah could obey, he received another greater commission: He was called to enter and abide in the ark. Seven days before the Lord sent the raging flood to cover the earth, Noah and his family were sent inside the ark. Then God Himself brought the animals to him (Genesis 7:7–10). It was a miracle of migration.

Noah obeyed by abiding. He entered into the ark to abide and to rest in his salvation. As he did, God Himself performed what He had commanded. *The Lord fulfilled His own command to Noah.*

As Noah did, we fulfill God's great commission by abiding in Christ and allowing the Lord to bring them in. Those who abide in Jesus attract others to the Lord. To obey God is to abide in Christ—and God will fulfill what He has commanded us to do.

What is true for the Great Commission is true for every command. How wonderfully simple He makes it for us!

While others focus on forming committees and gathering

resources and formulating programs, we will abide in Jesus. If we abide in Him, He will bring the world to our feet.

Shout this secret from the housetops!

Yours in abiding in Christ . . .

24 | *Perfect Peace over Your Imperfect Past*

Dear Beloved by God,

I was sorry to hear that memories and consequences of your inglorious past continue to interfere with your glorious present. I know you rejoice in your identification with the Lord Jesus Christ, and you know that in Him there is no condemnation. Still your history disturbs your present peace.

I write to tell you of a comfort that brought my heart relief when I fell victim to my past. I don't wish to add to your burden or to admonish you. You will not be helped by introspection; you won't be delivered from the past by delving deeper into the past in order to discover and remove supposed unresolved conflicts. You don't need partial and gradual healing such as that promised by those who have learned at the feet of Gamaliel.

When Israel was redeemed from the slavery of Egypt, the

nation was invited to rest in the Lord, to stand still and behold God's salvation. God assured them that He Himself would fight for them. He called them to the simplicity of faith.

For God's redeemed people, Egypt represented the past. Although God had defeated Egypt through the ten plagues, Pharaoh still had an army capable of pursuing Israel. In other words, while Egypt was their defeated enemy in regard to the *doctrine* of God's salvation, it was an undefeated enemy in regard to their *experience* of God's salvation. Egypt was behind Israel, but pursuing all the while.

We now know the end of the story, but Israel did not. So we can understand why they "became very frightened" (Exodus 14:10) to look back and see this formidable Egyptian army with its six hundred chariots rumbling at their heels. In this fear, they were running from their past. They were redeemed and running rather than redeemed and resting. They were running from Egypt, running from bondage—running from their history. Their past was not really past. Would it overtake them?

In their terror, "the sons of Israel cried out to the LORD" (14:10). How did God meet their need?

> *And the angel of God, who had been going before the camp of Israel, moved and went behind them; and the pillar of cloud moved from before them and stood behind them.*

How simple! The Lord placed Himself between Israel and Egypt. God places Himself between His children and their pasts so that when they look back, they see only Him. This is God's cure for dealing with yesterday.

Dear anxious friend, God wants you to enjoy perfect peace

about your imperfect past because you have a perfect Savior. The day will finally come for both of us, and for all of God's fretting children, when we shall stand on the victory side and see "every Egyptian dead on the seashore." Until that day arrives, let us never take our eyes off Him.

May the One who was the Glory of the cloud and is the Glory of your life go before you and settle brightly between you and your past.

Yours, ever gazing on the Lord . . .

25 | *God Gives You Complete Victory*

Dear Seeker after Truth,

Since you're praying for victory in your personal life, I believe it's appropriate to pass along to you the most concise description of victory I've found in the Bible. It's the Holy Spirit's words addressed to believers through the apostle Paul: "Death is swallowed up in victory" (1 Corinthians 15:54). Here God declares victory over man's most unsolvable problem: death. He wants us to claim and enjoy this victory at all times.

If medical science were to announce that a life-threatening disease had been "swallowed up in victory," we would understand that the disease had been halted in its tracks and would never again afflict people. Its power to leave families ravaged and bereaved had been broken. The cure would ensure there would be no more victims; the disease was dead.

The victory the Lord Jesus declares over death is greater than any victory over disease. A medical cure would have no power to undo the damage and destruction of life that the disease had already caused. But Christ's complete victory over death not only halts the problem in its tracks, it also undoes all the damage it has ever caused. By His glorious resurrection Jesus has guaranteed a victory that reaches not only into the unending future, offering life to all, but also backward into human history—all the way back to Adam—promising to undo all the ruin death has ever wrought.

Such a victory so complete that it can reanimate the scattered dust of kingdoms and the ashes of the billions who have lived is the same sort of victory you seek.

It means this:

All things are possible with God;
His arm is strong, His will is free.
Now since He lives within my heart
All things are possible for me!

Rest in His rest and claim His most complete victory. Believe that the Lord will not only put a rapid end to all that hinders your sight of Him, but will also reverse the curse and bring forth light from the thickest darkness. A victory which extinguishes the fire but does not rebuild the house falls short of the victory that swallows up death. Remember how when God cured Naaman's leprosy, He restored the man's flesh like that of a young healthy child (2 Kings 5:14).

The enemy would love for you to settle for a partial victory. In every problem, embrace the wonderful truth that "death is swallowed up in victory." Honor the Lord by claiming and enjoying a victory made complete by His finished work and glorious resurrection. You have been declared complete in Him; let faith insist on His complete victory.

Yours, in His complete victory . . .

26 | *Your Incentive for Holiness*

To the Lamb's Bride,

You have posed a difficult question: "What is your greatest incentive to live a holy life?"

I've thought deeply about my answer. My greatest incentive for living a holy life is the conviction that God reveals His Husband-heart to His holy bride. The holier I am, the more I can enter into the revelation of God as Husband. Let me explain.

The revelation of Christ as the Bridegroom of the soul is the consummating revelation. Everything moves toward the expression of the Husband-heart of God. All the other revelations of Christ prepare me for this revelation.

For example, if I desire to know the Lord as my Shepherd, I will come to Him as a dumb sheep; if I desire to know Him as Redeemer, I must humbly present myself to Him as a guilty sinner.

The penniless beggar in rags has the greatest chance to know Him as Provider; the incurably ill, as the great Physician. His glory as an Advocate is revealed to the guilty whom He freely represents; He becomes a Friend to the friendless and a Refuge to all who helplessly cry out to Him.

Every revelation of the Lord Jesus is offered to the empty hand. Our deficiency qualifies us to appropriate His adequacy. Our need opens the door to His supply. We come to Him dumb and dirty, blind, helpless, and guilty. The greater our need, the more beautiful our Savior appears to us.

But there is one grand exception. To experience the outflowing of the love of our Heavenly Groom, we must come to Him as *His holy bride*. The holier our hearts—the more conformed to Christ, the more complete and mature—the more the Husband-heart of God will be revealed.

Do you understand why so few know the Lord Jesus in this way? Because holiness is so far from us. To know Him as Groom I do not come in deficiency, but in maturity. That is why the Holy Spirit is so intent on conforming us to Christ. Only conformity to Christ allows God to manifest His Husband-heart.

I am not suggesting we should stop approaching Him in our need and natural poverty. But the secret passage to His most intimate revelations is identification with, and conformity to, the resurrection and sufferings of Jesus. This, and this alone, opens His Husband-love to our souls.

I would never urge you to seek holiness as a goal; the goal is Christ—always only Christ! Holiness is the means to understanding God's Husband-heart. The jealous love of God will never leave us alone. God longs to show us what a wonderful

Groom and Husband He really is. From the moment we first laid believing eyes on Him, God has been at work in our souls, laboring, shaping, polishing, pruning, and ruling and overruling every detail of our lives so that we could experience Him as the Husband of our souls.

By creed we have His Husband-heart in prospect; by faith we have His Husband-heart as a present possession.

My personal passion for holiness has never been greater since I discovered that holiness is the key that allows Him liberty to open His Husband-heart to me as He desires. There are other incentives to holiness to be sure, but for me this is the highest.

Yours, in pursuit of the Groom's heart . . .

27 | *A Higher Goal Than Holiness*

Dear Child of the Covenant,

I share your great desire to be holy as God is holy, but I do not share your zeal in pursuing holy things. Holiness isn't a goal to pursue; it is a by-product. The goal of our heart must ever be the Lord Himself.

You well know how the discovery of Christ and the message of the New Covenant has already implanted a desire for holiness in your heart. Fruit belongs not to those who earnestly seek it, but to those who seek Jesus. No holiness can be found outside faith's possession of the Lord Jesus Christ and no partaking of holiness without partaking of the Holy One.

Jesus is holy, and every call for us to be holy is another invitation to appropriate the Lord Himself. A world of frustration belongs to those who attempt to "do" holy. We can be holy, but we cannot do holy. Holiness has to do with character—*His* character.

The book of Haggai wonderfully illustrates this truth. The newly emancipated slaves from Babylon, in their great desire to please the Deliverer, were sorely tempted to run after holiness by their contact with holy things. The prophet responded by pointing out that food does not become holy merely by being touched by something holy, but the same food would become defiled if it touched something unclean.

Are we more holy if we stand in the company of the saints? Does partaking of the holy ordinances sanctify us? If we study the Book of God without ceasing, can our contact with the Bible make us holy?

The Scriptures are the well, not the water. Christ Himself is the Water of Life.

I would never want to hear that you had neglected prayer, fasting, stewardship, corporate worship, music, the Table, the Book, the altar, or missions and evangelism and the wonderful works of charity. But we must remember the priest's ruling. We are not made holy by touching holy things.

Imagine a person in Haggai's day reasoning this way: *I desire to become holy. The holiest place on earth is the Holy of holies. I will trespass the holy veil and stand in the holiest place of all. I will stand in the Holy of holies in the presence of the symbolic throne of God and in the light of the shekinah glory cloud!* What would have happened to that man? He would have been incinerated in a sudden flash. By touching the holy place he would not have been sanctified, but roasted.

My friend in Christ, let us run after Jesus who is the fountain of life and holiness. We do not need to touch holy things; we need no manuals on holy living; we certainly do not need to chase after fruit.

Our fellowship with Jesus will certainly bring us into continual contact with holy things, but our contact with holy things will never bring us into fellowship with Him.

I love you and would spare you needless torment. I pray you would consider the priest's ruling.

While there's breath in my body,
While there's reason in my soul,
While there's life in my spirit,
The Lord will be my goal!

Sanctified in Him, I remain yours . . .

28 | *God's Voice Gives Life to His Word*

Dear Hearing Heart,

I commend your earnest desire to be thoroughly grounded in the Word of God. We are all responsible before God to "hold fast the form of sound words."

Many neglect the precious Word of God altogether. They have no theology, no doctrine, no objective revelation of truth.

Others, I fear, are legalistic about biblical truth. They have an extensive and profound knowledge of the Scriptures, but their hearts are barren and their creed leaves them cold and formal.

How can we be liberated on the one hand from no creed at all, and on the other from a frozen dogma that imparts no freshness or vitality to our hearts?

Dear friend, may the good Lord help us perceive the organic union between the Word of God and the voice of God. By the

Word of God I mean the revelation of God in the person of the Lord Jesus in the Scriptures. The Bible is the Word of God. The voice of God which comes through the Word of God is also a revelation, an illumination. It is a revelation of the revelation.

The Word of God is objective; the voice of God is subjective. The voice of God is the special revelation of the Lord Jesus in the Bible brought home by the Holy Spirit to our hearts.

The voice of God in the Word of God makes the Bible "living and active and sharper than any two-edged sword." The naked Scriptures alone do not search the spirit, dividing joints and marrow and the thoughts and intentions of the heart. It is the voice of God that unveils the Christ of the Bible, and says to us (in Hebrews 3),

Today, if you hear His voice, do not harden your hearts.

If we would indeed be grounded in the Word of God, we must become increasingly sensitive to the voice of God. Bible memory, systematic study, extensive research, or a workable knowledge of the original languages will never by themselves impart a warm and living creed; only the voice of God can do that. God must speak through His Word by the Holy Spirit of truth, who reveals and glorifies the Lord Jesus by taking what is His and making it known to us (John 15:26, 16:13–14).

There is life only in Him who is the Truth. If we are grounded in His voice, we will be grounded in His Word.

Can you imagine a greater tragedy than having His Word and missing His voice? But for those who hear His voice, life is an Emmaus Road. His voice inflames the heart. The revelation of Him in all the Scriptures makes known to us His living orthodoxy.

King Solomon prayed for a hearing heart. May God grant this prayer for both of us. I know that you, as His true sheep, are hearing His voice and can say (in the words of Song of Solomon 5:2),

I was asleep, but my heart was awake. A voice! My beloved was knocking: "Open to me, my sister, my darling, my dove, my perfect one!"

Yours, ever listening for His voice . . .

29 | *His Heart Is the Key to His Words*

Dear Hungry Heart,

You asked if God's words would ever contradict His heart. No, never—but often His words appear to. Ultimately the King's words will express the King's heart, but often His words seem to take a long, winding path to get there.

If we know His heart, we can understand His words. I encourage you to interpret His words by your intimate knowledge of His heart. Let me illustrate this.

When King Solomon said, "Get me a sword. Divide the living child in two," his heart was proclaiming, "Save the baby!" He never intended to slay the infant (even though he commanded exactly that); he always planned to save the child.

In the same way it's possible for us to respond to God's words in a way that divides and destroys, altogether missing the loving intention of His heart. To understand the King's heart we must have from God in heaven a revelation, an illumination. Without this, His words will often be misunderstood and misapplied.

Unassisted scholarship can never, by itself, discover the King's heart. Unmeasured damage is done in the name of the King and the King's decree by trying to understand His words without discerning His heart. If we are to obey our Royal Savior, it must be by the light His heart sheds upon His lips.

Be a thorough student of the precious Word of God, my hungry friend, but be ever careful that you do not use the sword in such a way that you kill the baby. Take the sword; then rightly divide by daring to run with the King's heart. Do not fear the apparent contradiction between His heart and His lips. It is a paradox. Embrace His heart and you are safe. His heart is the key to His words.

This distinction can mean the difference between life and death. When you do not understand His words, run after His heart. If you have His heart, you will be enabled to understand His words.

Study, my diligent friend in Christ, study; but in all your studying, save the baby!

Yours, in the knowledge of God's heart . . .

30 | *Truth Is a Person*

Dear Seeker after Truth,

Because we are kindred spirits, I have the courage to express my concern over your recent passion for sound doctrine. God loves us too much to settle for sound doctrine in our lives. There is such a thing as barren orthodoxy, and I pray God would spare you from it. The heart will never be satisfied with dogma.

It is possible to have pure doctrine without seeing Jesus, but it isn't possible to truly behold the reality of Christ and embrace error. Truth is a Person; it is our Lord Jesus Christ. He is the only truth our poor hearts will ever need, and more abstract forms of truth can easily detract from Him. When we live in the revelation of the person of Christ, we must respond in reverent worship and fall at His precious feet. We cannot see the Truth and embrace a lie.

I'm impressed at the amazing doctrine of the Lord Jesus found in the gospel of John. The evangelist wrote of the wonder of being in union with God and having God in union with His people; he wrote of One called the Word who had no beginning, and of One who did not need to commit Himself to men because He knew what was in men.

By the Holy Spirit's inspiration, John wrote of the impeccable purity of the Lord Jesus and His awful authority. He depicted our Lord's priesthood and His royal crown. He gave to the sheep the Shepherd's assurance of the hand that secured them.

John's gospel is preeminently the gospel of the Glory of Christ. He spelled it all out for us in pure doctrine.

And then, when John on the Island of Patmos saw these same truths in the glorified person of Jesus, he fell down at His feet as a dead man.

I'm not suggesting that the apostle John had previously held these truths in unreality. He did not. However, there is a qualitative difference between knowing about the doctrine of the Lord's omniscience and beholding His eyes like a flame of fire; between having an orthodox view of His sovereignty and seeing a sharp, two-edged sword flash from His mouth; between declaring His glory in a creedal statement and beholding His face like the sun when it shines in full strength.

When John saw the Truth in the person of Jesus, he was humbled to the dust. It was far more than theology when John beheld the living, glorified Savior pervading His people and holding the representative elders in His hand.

I'm sure your desire for pure doctrine is healthy and a by-product of your living revelation of the Lord Jesus. But I would be dishonest before God if I didn't vent my burden and fear. Thank you for giving me this liberty.

May the Truth Himself fill you with a living creed, and may His warm vision keep your heart from a frozen theology.

Your friend in the Truth . . .

31 | *Touching His Garment and Touching Him*

Dear Fellow Believer,

I agree with you that the means through which we seek the Lord *may* hinder fellowship with Him—but they need not. As the woman in Mark 5 discovered, it is possible to touch the Lord Jesus Christ by touching His garment. If she had touched only the garment that day and not the Lord, she would have received no more relief than she had from the physicians for twelve years.

Here on earth we do not touch Him directly, but only through the garment, the channel, the means. (Though we read of a day when believers "shall see His face" and "He shall dwell among them" in a city where "the Lord God, the Almighty, and the Lamb are its temple" and we "serve Him night and day in His temple" [Revelation 21:3,22; 22:3–5; 7:15]. Imagine seeing His face directly! It is a marvelous mystery.) The garment represents any-thing through which we see the Lord.

Sometimes it is His creative handiwork. How many times have we beheld His eternal Godhead and power through the things He made? We have seen Him in the stars and in the storm; in the mountains and in the meadow; in the forests and by the sea—everywhere we have looked the Lord has been present. When we observed the birds and the flowers, we beheld Him. Nature is a grand garment through which we have touched the Savior.

Our Savior has many garments to help us touch Him. Even the written Word of God is in a sense a garment through which we reach the Lord. Fellowship with like-minded hearts, prayer, stew-ardship, baptism, the breaking of bread—all these redemptive pic-tures help us stretch our faith toward God.

So garments need not hinder our union with the Lord. How-ever, it's possible to touch the garment and miss the Lord. Many earnest believers embrace the picture in such a way that they com-pletely miss the Painter. Bible study, for example, is a wonderful thing if Christ is in it, but if He is not, it leads to spiritual pride. Prayer without Christ is powerless. Fellowship with believers is a great blessing if the Lord is in it, but if He isn't, how quickly it de-generates into an empty garment. Music may be a wonderful channel of worship and praise if the Lord is present, but what a lifeless garment it is if He is absent.

We must not despise the many instruments God provides to enable us to touch Him by faith. But we must never settle for the garment alone. The brass serpent Moses set up in the wilderness served as a garment through which snake-bitten sinners touched the Lord and found salvation. But the same garment later became *nehushtan* (only a piece of brass) and had to be destroyed because God's people began to venerate the picture and forgot the Lord (2 Kings 18:4).

Until we stand before Him in our resurrected and glorified bodies, we will always touch our Savior through various means. But He knows that when we touch the hem of His garment we are reaching out for Him, and in this we rejoice. Let us determine together to touch no garment that does not contain Him.

Rest! Enjoy! Abide!

Your friend and servant . . .

32 | *Your Perfectly Suitable Savior*

Dear Unique Child of God,

Are you enjoying the fact that our Lord's adequacy perfectly suits the infinite variety of our needs and the uniqueness of our personalities? We may always come to Him wherever we are and trust Him to meet us there in flawlessly suitable grace, and to take us forward in our union with Him.

It's not as if the Lord has ten balms for ten wounds, forty solutions for forty problems, one hundred provisions for one hundred needs. His suitableness is far more wonderful. He may have one hundred balms for the same wound! For the same cry He may answer in a thousand ways.

Remember Mary and Martha? These were two very different people who shared an identical problem at the same moment. They both mourned the loss of their brother, Lazarus. Both loved their brother and experienced the pain of his death; both expressed love and trust in the Lord. But Martha was Martha and Mary was Mary, and even though they shared the same sorrow, the Lord did not deal with them identically. He was suitable to both, but not in the same way.

Martha was the practical sister, full of common sense, always pouring herself out in loving service. She was self-controlled. To Martha, Jesus was her honored Guest, and on this occasion she desired from Him a conversation. She needed to talk. With her our suitable Lord carried on a dialogue about her brother, about the doctrine of the future resurrection of the body, and about the present revelation of Himself as the Resurrection and the Life.

To Mary, the Lord Jesus was her honored Host. Mary was quiet, more contemplative, and naturally as profound in sorrow as she was in joy. Mary did not want to talk. She couldn't speak, but spilled out her soul in agony and unutterable anguish. Mary could only weep, and Jesus wept with her.

With Martha, Jesus listens and talks. With Mary, Jesus weeps. Martha gained the Savior's ears; Mary gained the Savior's tears.

Both sisters were supplied in their hour of need by a personal revelation of a suitable Savior. Jesus has many ways to give Himself away, and He supplies the same needs differently.

I urge you to be cautious, my brother, and to walk softly before the Lord when you are privileged to counsel the needy. You may assure the earnest seeker of the Lord's suitableness and faithfulness and all-sufficiency, but be doubly careful before you dare predict how the Lord will reveal Himself and which cure He will prescribe. The Lord is ever surprising us by the variety of His visitations. In the Gospel record this is certainly evident, for example, in the many ways Jesus healed blind men.

In your great desire to recommend the Savior to those who need Him, do not limit Him to the ways you've personally experienced Him. Proclaim Him as the suitable Savior, and allow Him room to meet them in a way that perfectly suits every individual. He knows all about each and every one of us.

Enjoying His fullness . . .

33 | *When Christ Doesn't Seem Enough*

Dear Encourager of Faith,

I've found a Bible story that perfectly illustrates the point you made in your last letter about "embracing the objective fact of His glorious sufficiency."

I was reminded of Christ's miracle of feeding the five thousand. The apostle Andrew, holding in his hand the little boy's lunch that he had located as he brought it obediently to Jesus, must have entertained the thought, *This doesn't feel like it will be enough.* How insignificant the morsels must have seemed in this fisherman's large and powerful hands. Even as that food was being miraculously multiplied, and as Andrew went back and forth from Jesus' feet to the hungry multitude, he may have wondered at the seeming futility of the task before him. Yet at every moment the small amount of food he held in his hand symbolized the all-sufficiency of the Bread of Life Himself.

You have accurately pointed out that "it never feels like we have enough of Jesus." It probably didn't feel like enough for Andrew. If we would take the time and look over our shoulders and rehearse in our hearts the vast amount of provision we have already distributed, we would be humbled to think that we ever doubted His sufficiency. If the apostle Andrew had to carry all at once the amount of food he eventually distributed, he would have been crushed under the load.

As far as the Lord is concerned, we must not waste a millisecond of concern on what the natural eye can see or the physical hand can feel. Jesus is the all-sufficient supply for us, and through us to others. He so portions Himself to us that in sharing Him with others we discover that He is everlastingly enough. God wisely keeps us always returning to Him for more. At the moment it may not look or feel like sufficiency, but when the distribution is reckoned, we will see to our everlasting joy how perfect was the supply.

We will never run out of Jesus. We must never fear to have the multitude assemble before us to be fed. It is God's wonderful way with us that we continually give until we are empty and then return to Him for a fresh supply of Jesus. The all-sufficiency of Jesus makes a mockery of sight; it is too grand for anything but faith.

Deliver us from sight and sense
And what appears to be,
That faith may sink a well in Him
Who is sufficiency!

Remember, your capacity isn't great enough to hold the Christ you have already given away.

And thank you for feeding me!

Yours, in His sufficiency . . .

34 | *All God's Commands Are Invitations*

Dear Servant of the Living Lord,

You must not crucify yourself for your inability to meet the high standards of God's holy law. The work of crucifixion has always been His and not ours, and it has long been finished.

I too have wrestled with my flesh and have prayed—wrongly—that God would grace me to obey. We do not need to pray for this because we have the will already. Nor should we pray that the Lord will empower us and make us adequate to perform His will, for He is our adequacy. He will never make us adequate apart from Him.

I *will* pray—earnestly—that the Lord will give you eyes to see His heart and purpose in commanding His children.

Why does God request of us things that are beyond our capacities? We may be certain that it isn't to mock or frustrate us.

Why then does He require us to walk in His ways? If God doesn't expect obedience from us, why does He issue commands?

Perhaps we can gain a little insight by examining in John 4 the command He gave the woman at the well.

There came a woman of Samaria to draw water. Jesus said to her, "Give Me a drink."

The Lord Jesus was thirsty, but not merely for water. His physical thirst illustrated His heart-thirst for a spiritual relationship with this woman. She was the one who really thirsted, and He was the one with real water.

When Jesus said to her, "Give Me a drink," He intended for her to recognize her need for spiritual water. He longed to give this woman Living Water. He wanted her to partake of Him and His salvation so she would bask in His satisfying fullness. By commanding her to give Him water, He was inviting her to request water from Him. His command was an invitation. And He knew that if she responded to it, she would never thirst again but would have a spring of everlasting life in her heart.

Jesus wanted her to ask Him for the very thing He had commanded of her. He commanded her so that she would want what He commanded.

Though the Lord Jesus did not receive from her one drop of water to quench His thirst, His deeper thirst was satisfied. This woman responded to His invitation, and Jesus gave her the water He had commanded her to give Him. Jesus was glad to fulfill His command in her.

All of God's commands are invitations to ask Him for the very thing He has required of us. When He commands us to turn the other cheek, or to go the second mile, or to consider it all joy when we encounter various trials, or to forgive one another, He is inviting us to receive from Him the very thing He has commanded. Whatever His command may be, He tells us to do so that He may do for us.

Every command is a promise of what He desires to work in us.

We are the only ones surprised when we fail to obey God's commands—He is not. Only the Lord Jesus can live the Christian life. While others punish themselves for falling short of His glory, we can rejoice in the gospel and approach Him on New Covenant ground.

In this world thirst seeks for water; in the spiritual world the Water has sought out the thirst.

Dear friend in Christ, Jesus is thirsty—so drink deeply.

In His faithfulness . . .

35 | *Victory Is More Than Defeating the Enemy*

Dear Heir of Christ,

I can well understand your feeling troubled that after knowing Jesus this long, you still have such corruption in your heart. You wonder why God doesn't drive out every enemy in one blow so that you might enjoy victory. Perhaps you'll find some light in the encouraging words God gave His redeemed people through Moses:

> *And the LORD your God will clear away these nations before you* little by little; *you will not be able to put an end to them quickly, lest the wild beasts grow too numerous for you.*
> (Deuteronomy 7:22)

> *I will drive them out before you* little by little, *until you become fruitful and take possession of the land.* (Exodus 23:30)

God longs to give us the land and all it symbolizes. The Israelites' possessing of the land of milk and honey was only a shadow of what it means to possess the Lord Jesus Christ, the bubbling fountain of living milk and honey.

We are to possess Christ! That is God's will for us. Rest and victory come when we possess Him.

And our hearts might easily focus on possessing "the land" in this way, if we had no Canaanites—if we had no enemies in the form of our sins—to subdue and dispossess. Because of these Canaanites, it's easy for us vessels of clay to become sidetracked into wanting to annihilate them.

And our hearts are such that if we were to see every sin put down—if He immediately destroyed for us every selfish thought, every proud look, every move toward retaliation, every temptation—we would be deceived into believing we were living in victory.

But that is not victory, though many thousands are thus deluded. They chase after deliverance from sin yet never possess the Lord Himself.

How tragic to defeat sin, but remain a relative stranger to the wonder of Christ! What good is being delivered *from* Canaanites if we are not being delivered *unto* Jesus?

That is why God takes us forward little by little, gradually gracing us to possess the land He has already conquered for us. By refusing to annihilate the enemy in a single blow, God humbles us and keeps our eyes on Jesus. Sanctification will be ours by measure and degree. Little by little God will conquer sin for us until we claim the high ground of possessing Christ.

I am not worried that you struggle with temptations. I understand how this troubles you, but be assured that these temptations are God's instruments to keep you focused on Christ.

Look at it this way: If temptations drive you to Jesus, are they your enemy? Surely, by God's overruling power, your enemies are fighting for you!

If every Canaanite were driven from your life (glorious thought!) and yet you failed to possess the land prepared for you, your condition would be worse and not better. Instead of enjoying victory you would find your life overgrown with weeds and filled with wild and destructive beasts.

You would be like the house the Lord spoke of—swept but not filled. Such a house becomes the dwelling of a host of greater evils.

I want you to enjoy real victory, the victory that comes from possessing Christ and living in union with Him. Victory is a Person; victory is our Lord Jesus Christ.

God has spoken. We will struggle with Canaanites until we "become fruitful and take possession of the land." May God keep us both from wild beasts.

Your fellow heir in Christ . . .

36 | *He Will Test the Truth He Teaches You*

Dear Friend in Christ,

You ended your last letter by saying the Lord has taught you a wonderful truth which you'll tell me more of later. I look forward to learning about it.

Meanwhile, my dear friend, be certain that if the Lord has taught you a wonderful truth He will test that truth in your life. He loves His children too much to allow them to hold truth in unreality.

When the Lord Jesus miraculously fed the five thousand, He taught His disciples a lesson about His superabundant sufficiency. He allowed very little time before He tested their grasp of this lesson. Immediately following the miracle they were commanded to go to the other side of the sea by boat.

In the middle of the lake, in the darkest hour of the night,

God sent a wind that battered their boat. Had they learned what He wanted them to understand from the miracle of the loaves and fish? Would they appropriate His adequacy?

Mark informs us that their Teacher had departed to a mountain to pray during their test. No doubt He was praying that His students would apply the truth He had taught them that afternoon among the multitudes.

But instead of depending on the Lord's sufficiency, the disciples strove at the oars, trying to battle the elements and ride victoriously through the storm. When the Teacher saw them "straining at the oars," He drew near to them in His all-sufficiency, walking on the frothing water. Still testing them, He waited for them to ask for His all-sufficient help. They again failed the test of their faith, but the patient Teacher spoke and calmed the storm. Mark informs us that the twelve "had not gained any insight from the incident of the loaves."

I do not know what truth the Lord has taught you; I only know that He will test it. Do not be surprised if you find yourself in the midst of a storm. But remember you have nothing to fear. Should you fail the test of your faith and hold the truth as only an orthodox but detached creed, your patient Teacher will draw near and rescue you. He will teach and test repeatedly, as long as it takes, until we embrace Him in His adorable sufficiency. We may not learn quickly, but His patience guarantees that we will learn well.

As you tell me of your special insight, I'll be interested to hear of the storm as well. The Lord, your High Priest, is praying that you pass your test.

Your co-learner in Christ . . .

37 | *Ravens from Hell or from Heaven?*

Dear Discerning Friend in Christ,

You have rightly identified the seed-stealing birds in the parable Jesus told as "the evil one" who comes and "snatches away what has been sown." But the birds you described in your last letter seem more like Elijah's ravens from heaven than the birds of the enemy. As you know from the prophet Isaiah, God's thoughts are not our thoughts and His ways are not our ways. The heavens are closer to the earth than God's ways and thoughts are to ours. So it takes a miracle of God for us to see the difference between the birds of heaven and those of hell.

To the human eye, ravens look fearsome and threatening. Along with the other unclean birds listed in Leviticus 11, the raven is a scavenger, one of the last birds one would expect God to use. Ravens steal and devour provision (their diet is mainly carrion).

What a mighty miracle God performed when He commanded ravens, against their nature, to bring Elijah his daily bread.

Are you 100 percent certain, my friend, that the birds in your life have come to rob you? Or have they been sent from heaven? May God grace you to know the difference. It's understandable to believe that a raven has come to steal your goods, but often the eye of faith will see a wonderful blessing in the raven's beak.

Not every sickbed, hardship, adverse circumstance, or reversal is from the enemy. God often sends blessing-bearing ravens in the form of trouble and testing.

If from time to time God did not use the unclean instrument to deliver His grace, where would we be, unworthy instruments that we are?

If the birds have come to snatch away God's precious seed from your heart, take authority in the name of the Lord and drive them away, as Abraham faithfully drove away the birds that sought to devour God's provision (Genesis 15:11). But if they are sent from heaven to bring you nourishment, embrace them by faith as His mysterious instruments of blessing. The situation which causes such consternation may well bear the Lord's double blessing.

In His mysterious love . . .

38 | *Ministry Is Bringing Pleasure to His Heart*

Dear Lover of Jesus,

I know you were disappointed when that hoped-for door of ministry closed to you. But as you well know, there is a higher ministry, and your heart qualifies you in this service of love. Our Lord Jesus is delighted with whatever service we give Him out of love. Anything we do or say that ministers to His heart and pleases Him is biblical Christian service.

Meditate with me on the anointing that Mary of Bethany gave our Lord Jesus just before His crucifixion. Mark tells us that as Jesus was reclining at the table, she came and broke a "vial of very costly perfume of pure nard . . . and poured it over His head" (14:3). John tells us that she also "anointed the feet of Jesus, and wiped His feet with her hair; and the house was filled with the fragrance of the perfume" (John 12:3).

Mary's service appeared to be unwise and reckless. Those experienced in Christian stewardship thought it a waste of money; they said it would have been far wiser had she sold the perfume and given the money to the poor. They presumed to know what constituted Christian service. Mary had no formal training in Christian ministry, and they saw her as an embarrassment.

By her impetuous action, Mary did place Jesus in an embarrassing situation. It's possible that Jesus carried the aroma of her perfume with Him to the cross. He likely could not have removed the fragrance easily since it was in His hair, on His clothes, and rubbed into the skin of His feet. Even in that culture such an expensive perfume on the body of a man might raise questions about His masculinity or about who He had been lying with. Most men would instinctively recoil if someone should pour perfume on them.

To everyone but Christ, Mary's ministry must have seemed a failure. But the Lord wasn't embarrassed by her actions. He had no hard words for her. In fact, the reverse was true; He rebuked those who chided her.

He knew that Mary's intention was to minister to His heart. She had no other motive in mind; she threw all thought of cost or consequences to the wind. She wanted to express her love for Christ in an act of sacrificial love to Him, and He received it gratefully.

Mary offered the highest service possible: She ministered to the heart of the Lord Jesus.

I share this, my friend, so that you might never hold back the spontaneous impulses of love generated by a worshiping heart. Do not fear what others will think. Do not weigh the consequences.

Give no thought to the price you must pay. Do not think the Lord Jesus will be embarrassed by your radical service.

Ask only: Will this minister to Christ's heart? If so, do not hold back anything. Break all of your precious jars so that He might know you love Him.

And know this: A closed door does not disqualify an open heart. You have a wonderful ministry to render to a wonderful Savior.

The Lord Jesus deserves the best ointment we have. Do not count any service to His heart too small or too radical. Live only for His pleasure.

Yours, in the service of His heart . . .

39 | *Know Him, Not His Purposes*

Dear Beloved of the Lord,

After those words "What is God doing" in your last letter I delighted to see that you placed an exclamation point and not a question mark. We may wonder deeply, but we should never question defiantly. Your tone suggested you would be thrilled if God let you in on His wise designs in your life. Be patient. In due time you will know all you need to know. It is infinitely more important to know Him than it is to know His purpose in your life.

Yet I know your passion to know God's purpose and direction and will for you as He molds you into the image of His Son. You think it would be helpful to know the sort of vessel (and its use) into which He is skillfully and lovingly forming you.

But how does the clay come to know the Potter's heart? Not from study. It isn't doctrine that will instruct the clay in the mysteries of the Potter's heart. Only submission will do it. As the clay submits to the Potter, the Potter is free to work into the clay His heart and purpose.

Not that the Potter will announce His plan once the clay yields to His hand. If that were the case, you would have known His plan by now. Instead God silently works His purposes into the clay. The more submissive the clay, the more conformed it will become to the designs of the Potter. In that way the clay becomes His purpose without even knowing what it is.

The Potter has called us to know Him, not His purposes in us.

Trust Him without fear or reservation, my dear friend. The Potter's hands will not stretch, pound, pull, scrape, or apply pressure in vain. Nor does He delight in seeing us spin needlessly around the wheel. Every turn of the wheel and every pressure of His hand are wisely applied to our lives in His loving re-creation of us. He is working us from the inside out to conform us into vessels of honor. Wise love is forming us.

Let us not fear the turnings, the pressure, or the silence. Where the pressure is greatest the vessel will no doubt be most unique and the Potter most glorified.

The simplicity of this is awesome! We must know Him, not His purposes, and we know Him through submission.

Clay was never in better hands than the hands that now are molding you. Rest!

Yours, as clay in the Potter's hands . . .

40 | *Your Barren Womb*

Dear Spiritual Friend,

I rejoice in your emphasis on grace. God can and will accomplish all that He has promised. We may rest forever in that reality.

But remember also that the very grace that claims, "God can!" also declares, "We cannot!" Some have embraced His adequacy without acknowledging their own inadequacy and have therefore miscarried in the work of the Lord.

Abraham, the father of faith and friend of God, made a grave error when he took Hagar into his tent. He had two facts to deal with. First was God's wonderful promise that Abraham would father a redemptive seed. Second was the barren womb in the chosen mother of that promised seed. Abraham's and Sarah's decision that he lie with Hagar was intended to foster God's promise, but it was also an attempt to circumvent the barren womb.

The same situation is true for us. It isn't enough to know that God has given great and precious promises; we must also realize that our womb is closed, and without a miracle we cannot bear fruit for God. The promise of God and the barren womb must always be embraced together. He must perform. I cannot.

Abraham and Sarah may have meant well, but the fruit of Abraham and Hagar's unhappy union has ill consequences to the present day.

I have no doubt you know this well, but some who are running with all of their might after the promise of God are sure to stumble over their own feet. They need to hear in words plain and simple that the Lord doesn't need our help. Every attempt to circumvent the barren womb is interference with His wonderful plan. How often we hinder God by trying to help Him.

Resist, by God's undeserved grace, every temptation to take Hagar into your tent. All that God has promised to do, He will perform without Hagar.

Remember too that it is not God's promise *plus* our programs or gifts or resources or efforts. The Lord has many times used those things as instruments of blessing, but always through the barren womb.

I pray you won't read into this letter a spirit of criticism. I've been badly burned by the flesh in my chase after the pure grace of God, and I would spare you the same agony.

May God touch your womb and may your fruit remain. Ever proclaim the grace of God!

Depending on Him for all . . .

41 | *Your Key to Discernment*

Dear Discerner of Truth,

This week I witnessed "signs and wonders" that made my spirit heavy and left my heart cold. I do not want to limit God or prejudge His messengers, but neither do I want to be deceived by that which appeals to my flesh and is observed with physical sight. Satan may be able to pull the wool over the eyes, but he is not able to pull wool over the heart that loves the Lord Jesus.

To determine if a prophet is true or false, there is a more spiritual test than whether his prophecy is fulfilled. A prophet may predict an event and provide many convincing evidences and wonders and yet still be a false prophet. Moses warned about this.

> *If a prophet or a dreamer of dreams arises among you and gives you a sign or a wonder, and the sign or the wonder comes*

true . . . you shall not listen to the words of that prophet or that dreamer of dreams; for the LORD your God is testing you to find out if you love the LORD your God with all your heart and with all your soul. (Deuteronomy 13:1–3)

How are we to discern the true from the false? There is nothing higher, deeper, more noble or spiritual, than to love the Lord your God with all your heart and with all your soul. We should not ask, "Does this prophet's prediction come true?" but, "Does the prophet's word or vision foster my love for the Lord Jesus? Does this person encourage me to love the Lord with all my heart and soul?"

This question is the heart-test of all reality. If something does not promote my devotion to the Lord, I should forsake it, no matter how true it appears. Signs and wonders that turn our hearts merely to signs and wonders are destructive. Sight is a poor guide in spiritual discernment. Sight by itself cannot discover the wolf in sheepskin; neither can it discern the enemy when he appears as the shepherd.

We must listen to those whose words help us to love Jesus. We must fellowship with those whose company encourages a more profound love for the Lord. We must read the books that take us forward in our intimate union with Christ. And we must be willing to reject every dream, wonder, sign, vision, prophecy, communication—anything—that doesn't draw us into a deeper love of Jesus.

Does it aid me in loving Jesus? This is the supreme test for discernment.

If you have a word that has helped you love Jesus more, please pass it along.

Yours in the Truth . . .

42 | *He Is Always Willing to Forgive Your Sin*

Dear Brother in Christ,

Thank you for sharing from your deepest heart the things you've learned in meditating on the miracles of our Lord Jesus.

I'm happy to comment on your conclusions. I'll home in on one particular application you shared because I fear that your spirit, so sensitive to offending your glorious Lord, drew condemnation from a passage that was actually designed to minister unspeakable comfort to your soul.

You made very perceptive observations concerning the redemptive aspects of Jesus' healing ministry. In many ways disease does illustrate sin. I can certainly see how leprosy would represent the defilement and corruption of sin; palsy, the paralysis of sin; blindness, deafness, and fever, the debilitating consequences of sin. Our Lord Jesus Himself claimed that by calling sinners to repentance He was acting as a spiritual physician.

Perhaps more than we realize, all the physical miracles of our Lord were designed to illustrate some spiritual reality. His absolute authority, not only over disease but over demons, death, and nature as well, quickens us to believe that He has absolute authority over human nature. Your approach is a sound method of examining this wonderful part of our Savior's life and ministry.

But I wonder if your reading of our Lord's comment in Mark 1 to the man full of leprosy will stand in the light of the balance of Scripture? When Jesus says, "I am willing; be cleansed," do you really think it implied that there are some sins He isn't willing to forgive? He has not promised to heal every disease, but He is infinitely willing to forgive every sin.

That's one reason my heart goes out in sympathetic love to those who call their sin a sickness or a disease. They seek the sympathy of men and desire to secure a cure from science. They wrongly think that they have more hope by calling their moral addiction a disease. But if only they could see the heart of God! Then they would know that their true hope is in coming to Him as a moral leper. He will always say, "I am willing; be cleansed!"

There is far more hope in coming to the Lord as a sinner, for He will never deny—in fact He will not even delay—the cleansing of a sinner's heart.

I agree that with any disease it's appropriate to come before Him and say, "Lord, if You are willing, You can make me clean!" That's because we do not know His high purposes in those things. At times, for some wise design, He may let the cup pass; at other times, for a wise purpose, He may require us to drink it. He may heal me of disease; He may not.

But it doesn't follow that when we sin we must pray, "Lord, if you are willing—" as if He may not be. I believe He selected that man full of leprosy to ask the question once, so that we may know His heart forever: "I am willing; be cleansed!"

If we fall a thousand times, we will never hear Him say, "This time I am unwilling to cleanse you." No matter how great the offense, how deep the dye, how advanced our case of moral leprosy, we have a Savior who is willing at once to forgive us thoroughly. Oh, dear friend in Christ, we have in the Lord Jesus such a wonderful Advocate with the Father! It makes my spirit dance for joy.

Do look for the spiritual nuggets illustrated by the glorious miracles of the Lord Jesus, but hold them up to the light of the balance of Scripture. One truth will never contradict another.

We must be careful not to draw conviction from passages designed to bless us, nor must we draw comfort from Scriptures designed to bring us to repentance.

Study on, my brother, and thank you for inviting me to feast at your table. I pray that in all respects you may prosper and be in good health, just as your soul prospers. Rest!

In union with Jesus . . .

43 | *Let Him Serve You*

Dear Lover of Truth,

Thank you for inviting me to your conference. I plan to attend if the Lord wills.

You asked me to comment on the theme for this year's gathering: "Saved to Serve the Lord." If I may, I would like to raise it up and slide a foundation under it. It would be more accurate to proclaim, "Saved to Be Served by the Lord, in Order to Serve Him." Before we can lift a finger to serve the Lord, He is already serving us; before we can be givers, we must be receivers.

It would be a tragedy to inspire those in attendance to serve, then send them out powerless. It would be far better and more productive to first remind them of God's gracious heart. Before He commands us to wash our brother's feet, He washes our own.

Peter, who represents us in many ways, had to submit to this living principle before he could serve the Lord. Peter did not feel it was right for the Lord of heaven to bear the slave's towel and wash the feet of His servants. After all, should not the creature serve the Creator? Should not the servant wash the feet of the Master? No wonder Peter was so dogmatic, so intense: "Never, even into the ages of eternity [for such is the force of the Greek word he used] shall You wash my feet!"

Peter had not grasped that "the Son of Man did not come to be ministered unto, but to minister." Peter thought surrender meant, "I am saved to serve the Lord. I'll do anything for Him at any time, anywhere, at any cost. I need only be informed of His will and I'll hasten to wash His blessed feet." But before he could serve, Peter needed to understand he was redeemed by the Lord to first be served by Him. Then, in loving response, he could serve the Lord and others.

I worship every time I reflect on the words our Lord Jesus spoke to Peter: "If I do not wash you, you have no part with Me."

No part? Such solemn words! I doubt if the Savior was threatening the apostle with eternal loss, but He certainly was warning him of the possibility of missing out on deep and intimate fellowship. Jesus knew that ministry had to overflow from a heart refreshed from heaven.

I've already begun to pray for your conference, that the Lord will open wide every window, that the stale air we're so accustomed to breathing (our ministry to Him) might be replaced by the fresh and vitalizing Spirit of the truth that God desires to serve us.

If we allow Him to first minister *unto* us—to refresh us—there is little doubt that a great, refreshing gale will follow *through* us.

I hope this suggestion finds receptive soil in the hearts of those organizing the gathering.

I look forward to seeing you at the footwashing!

Yours, in His refreshment . . .

44 | *Fear the Dregs, and Welcome Changes*

Dear Faithful Servant of the Lord,

I'm happy to hear that God has given you a new responsibility. This need not be a burden to you or your family. Undoubtedly this will bring many changes: less time and energy and a strain on your resources. Do not regret these changes nor long for the day when God will make things as they were before. He may never do that. But do not fear. Changes are necessary for our spiritual health; otherwise we would become complacent and presumptuous, living under the same conditions year after year.

You're absolutely safe in the care of Him who cannot change and who has engineered your changes. God allows them to keep you focused on Himself.

A good illustration of this is found in God's reason for judging the land of Moab. He compares Moab to undisturbed wine settling on its dregs:

Moab has been at ease since his youth; he has also been
undisturbed on his lees, neither has he been emptied from vessel
to vessel, nor has he gone into exile. Therefore he retains his
flavor, and his aroma has not changed. (Jeremiah 48:11)

After grapes were crushed and strained through a sieve, what remained was poured into a large jar and allowed to sit. After a time, sediment would settle to the bottom, and the juice would be slowly and carefully poured off into another vessel. This process would be repeated until only the pure juice of the grape remained.

As a nation, Moab had not been poured from vessel to vessel. Instead, Moab had been "at ease." It had not been purified through pouring but had the unpleasant taste and aroma of the dregs.

Dear friend in Christ, our Lord Jesus loves us too much to allow us to become stale and settled and at ease. He will pour us from one vocation to another, from one location to another, from one circle of friends to another, from one crisis to another, from one health to another, from one responsibility to another. We will be poured back and forth from prosperity to adversity, from the familiar to the unfamiliar, from success to defeat, from peace to turmoil, until we become like Jesus.

The Lord knows we need changes, and He knows the changes we need.

And He knows that without changes we will not trust Him.

I pray you will enjoy your new duties. Love life! Remember that you will not be long in any condition. God is dealing with you as He does with all those He loves. Do not fear the experience of being poured back and forth; rather, fear the dregs, and long to be forever rid of them.

In His faithfulness . . .

Letters
of Rest

45 | *God Keeps You for Jesus*

Dear Secure One in the Lord,

You aren't the first to pose the question about the eternal security of a believer. The reason I skirt the question is not that I lack firm convictions, but because the question seems off-center and can lead a tender soul to a false sense of security.

By asking, "Do you believe in the doctrine of eternal security?" one may be led to believe that the safety of the child of God depends on a doctrine. We are not kept safe by any doctrine of eternal security; we are kept safe by God Himself. The Rock of our security is in the unchanging character of God. He will be faithful to keep us. His vows are upon us. We must never get sidetracked into thinking that some impersonal and abstract theology will keep us from backsliding or apostasy. The Lord alone keeps us and restores our souls. Our safety rests entirely on Him.

Old Testament believers refreshed their souls by singing this encouraging truth in Psalm 121—

He will not allow your foot to slip; He who keeps you will not slumber. Behold, He who keeps Israel will neither slumber nor sleep. The Lord is your keeper.

The closing benediction in the book of Jude also places the glory of our security squarely where it belongs:

Now to Him who is able to keep you from stumbling, and to make you stand in the presence of His glory blameless with great joy, to the only God our Savior, through Jesus Christ our Lord, be glory, majesty, dominion and authority, before all time and now and forever. Amen.

This is the first part of the truth in which your soul can rest. You're being kept by God Himself. You're as safe as His ability and determination to keep you.

Jude's letter begins with a slightly different aspect of our security:

Jude, a bond-servant of Jesus Christ, and brother of James, to those who are the called, beloved in God the Father, and kept for Jesus Christ.

The book that ends with the truth "kept by" begins with the truth "kept for." God not only keeps us, He keeps us for the Lord Jesus Christ. This is designed to flood our hearts with a river of peace. We have no intrinsic value in ourselves; we are being kept. Our value comes only from our identification with Christ and is realized by our union with Him.

If a dearly loved friend placed in your care an object of sentimental value and asked you to keep it for him, would you not treasure that object? You would do so because you treasure the one for whom you're keeping it. The object itself might be worthless, but it becomes precious because you're keeping it for someone you love.

We are being kept by God. We are being kept for the Lord Jesus Christ. Oh, how safe and secure the believer is! As precious as the Lord Jesus is to God the Father, so great is our safety in Him, for we are being kept safe for Him.

I do not know whether your question was prompted by a curiosity to know my position on the issue or because of doubt in your own soul whether you're eternally safe in Jesus. If you trust a doctrine, you may find yourself wondering whether you've fulfilled your part of any conditions connected with it. Or you may become presumptuous, thinking that by the doctrine of security God has painted Himself into a corner, thus allowing you to live recklessly. Some actually believe that the doctrine of eternal security must keep them heaven-bound no matter how they choose to live. God has no choice (they reason) but to save them, because He is bound by the doctrine.

May God deliver you from all doubts and quicken your union with Him. Our rest is in a Person, not in a doctrine.

You'll arrive safely because you are being kept by God for Jesus.

Yours, safe in Jesus . . .

46 | *Be a Grace-Pilgrim*

Dear Fellow Pilgrim,

Thank you for asking what I meant by the expression *grace-pilgrim* in my recent message to the believers meeting in your home. It's my pleasure to unfold so precious a topic.

Allow me to illustrate the concept before I define it. By bringing two different Bible stories together we have a perfect description of the grace-pilgrim.

The first concerns a wonderful miracle God performed for His children during their wilderness wanderings, and it is recorded in the Bible three times (Deuteronomy 8:4, 29:5; Nehemiah 9:21):

> *Your clothing did not wear out on you . . . your sandal has not worn out on your feet . . . nor did your feet swell these forty years.*

The more one meditates on the wonder of God's preserving the shoes and clothing of more than two million people for forty years and protecting their feet from swelling in their arduous trek over desert sand, the more one marvels at the Lord Himself. Those who are accustomed to standing or walking for many hours can testify how natural it is for their feet and ankles to hurt and swell. It was as supernatural an act for God to watch over their clothing and feet as it was for Him to part the Red Sea.

The second illustration is the story of the deception of the Gibeonites recorded in Joshua 9. God had commanded His people to act as His executioners against the sinful denizens of the land of Canaan. They were commanded to annihilate, without mercy, the seven nations coexisting there.

The Gibeonites were Hivites. So frightened were they of God's power and so certain of their own deserved destruction that they decided to deceive Joshua and his army into thinking they were only pilgrims passing through Canaan. By this plot they tried to exempt themselves from the threatened judgment. Their disguise was impressive. Their garments looked old and worn, they carried dried and parched wineskins and decaying sacks of stale and mildewed bread, and worn and weathered shoes covered their feet.

Their scheme succeeded because God's children lacked spiritual insight. Their pilgrim appearance fooled Joshua into making an unholy alliance.

The Gibeonites were not grace-pilgrims, but sight-pilgrims. They were acting for their very lives. It was essential that their costumes be convincing and that they be regarded as having trekked from a far-off country. They appealed to what could be seen with the eye—their clothing, their food, their drink, and their shoes—

all directed toward the flesh. From an earthly perspective the more worn, torn, patched, and weather-beaten the garments, the more solid the evidence for their long and difficult pilgrim journey.

On the other hand, Israel illustrated the grace-pilgrim. A grace-pilgrim is a Christian who has actually been through tough times but shows no negative evidence at the end of the ordeal. In fact, the opposite would appear to be the case. Sight would say, "Look at that Christian. His life has been easy. Look at his clothes—not even wrinkled. Look at his feet—not at all swollen. He knows nothing of a long and difficult journey. This person isn't a pilgrim!"

A grace-pilgrim is a follower of the Lord Jesus who doesn't exhibit the signs of a hard pilgrimage. His brow is not set with heavy furrows. His spirit does not manifest regret or weariness or defeat.

The grace-pilgrim is very much like Shadrach, Meshach, and Abednego after their fiery ordeal. Where was the smell of smoke? Where was their singed hair? Where was the charred clothing? They came through by grace, and therefore the signs and smells of the pilgrimage were not upon them.

The testimony of the grace-pilgrim is not one of survival but of Life. The world may speak of "grinning and bearing it," but God's ambassadors are sustained by the life and grace of God, and they march unscathed through the most impossible experiences.

Grace-pilgrims are ever rejoicing; they are prosperous; they live content and thankful; their clothes are ever new, their food is ever fresh, their strength is ever renewed. Their feet do not swell. Here is God's reputation in them: Not a note is heard of bitterness or complaint. This is the kind of grace God supplies to His pilgrims.

We will not be spared the hard places, my dear friend, but we are so often spared the natural consequences of the hard places.

May He grace both you and me with the beauty of the Grace-Pilgrim. His presence makes the yoke easy and the burden light.

Rejoicing in exile . . .

47 | *Your Fullness in Jesus*

Dear Cherished Teacher,

I was glad to hear that the flock you are shepherding has lambs as well as sheep. The spiritually young are so zealous for the many blessings found in Jesus. Yet they must not follow after "fullness" and in so doing miss the Savior.

We read in the book of Ruth that God taught Naomi the meaning of fullness—but she had to experience emptiness first. The Lord sent a famine, and she and her family thought they were empty. Though they had their family and sweet fellowship with God and the communion of saints, her husband uprooted them all, and they moved off covenant ground to enter a strange land.

In their search for fullness they ran into the very evil they had attempted to avoid. In Moab, Naomi buried her life partner and her children. After ten years of feeling empty, she finally realized how full she had been despite the famine; she had the Lord. She proclaimed: "I went out full, but the LORD has brought me back empty." When they began their quest to find fullness, she never dreamed she already was full.

When we have fellowship with Jesus, we are full even in a famine. How much better to be full with Christ, even in want, than to be prosperous yet empty without Him! Jesus is fullness; outside of Him is emptiness and illusion. I have seen many leave fullness in their attempt to find fullness—alas, I've sometimes led the way!—but I've returned as a bird to her nest.

I thrill at the green pastures you provide for your lambs. You have my continued intercession for your loving shepherding.

In union with the Great Shepherd . . .

48 | *God Gives What He Asks You to Gather*

Dear Resting One,

I'm so glad to hear your fresh insights into the grace of God that liberates us from having to work to obtain rest. Isn't God faithful to break the back of your anxiety and lead you into His rest? I share the exuberance of your joy.

And yet caution may be in order—not to dampen your joy but to deepen it.

By the grace of God we do not need to work *for* rest, but by the same grace we will be working by His Spirit *from* rest. What a glorious change of direction! God's rest is no longer a goal but a starting point. And from that starting point, faith is free to work by love.

I know you delight in the truth and you'll be thankful to be reminded that living faith is active. God has written this wonderful balance in all of nature.

They all wait for Thee, to give them their food in due season.
Thou dost give to them, they gather it up; Thou dost open Thy
hand, they are satisfied with good. (Psalm 104:27–28)

All living creatures depend on God for their supply. He gives; they gather. If He does not give, they gather in vain; if they do not gather, His giving is in vain. God doesn't drop the nut into the squirrel's mouth or the worm into the robin's beak. He will gladly give, but they must diligently gather.

Entering into God's rest empowers you to gather all that He gives you.

You will enjoy what dear sister Ruth discovered in the field of Boaz. By the free invitation and grace of Boaz, Ruth lived exclusively off the produce of his field. Boaz was the giver, but Ruth was required to gather—and gather she did. From sunrise to sunset, from the barley harvest in the spring, through the hot summer months and until the wheat harvest in the fall, she gathered.

Her daily gathering amounted to much more than would normally be realized from gleaning. She was no sluggard, but her bounty could not be explained by her gathering alone. Why were her dividends so great?

God allows us to peek behind the scenes into His heart to understand the secret of Ruth's prosperity. Boaz had commanded his field servants to drop handfuls on purpose for her to glean.

What a glorious picture of the blending of God's giving and man's gathering. Dear resting friend, so has it ever been. This is

God's way. I've experienced this principle in my study of God's Word. God must open my heart, He must illumine the Scriptures, He must reveal His Son, He must be the Giver—but this does not dismiss me from my responsibility to study diligently. I must do the donkey work. I must pour over the resources at my disposal and meditate upon the truth.

I have no doubt that just as Boaz knew the path Ruth would take and secretly dropped provision at her feet, so my Heavenly Boaz knows the path I will follow and He drops handfuls before me. I may gather all the day long, but if God does not drop secret supplies in front of me, I'll return empty from my gathering. We gather with the assurance that our gathering will not be in vain, because of the grace of God.

We cannot turn water into wine, but we must gather the water and fill the waterpots to the brim before God will do His miracle.

Gather, my resting friend, and know that all you gather He has graciously supplied. Do, do, do—not *for* rest, but *from* rest—then thank the Lord that He has secretly done, done, done.

God always provides what He requires us to gather. Ours is a gathering of grace.

Gather in rest!

In union with Jesus . . .

49 | *Prayer Is Laying Hold, Fasting Is Letting Go*

Dear Spiritual Friend,

I appreciate your desire to lay hold of living principles. I pray I can fulfill your request and show you the vital truth in fasting.

Our Lord linked prayer and fasting to illustrate the spiritual heart that lays hold of God even as it releases its grip on this present world system. True prayer clings to the Lord; true fasting refuses to hold on to the world.

A wonderful passage that illustrates the power of spiritual prayer and fasting is recorded in three of the Gospels. The Lord's disciples had recently returned from a dynamic ministry in which God had demonstrated His great power through signs and wonders. They had moved from village to village, healing diseases and exercising authority over demons (Mark 6:13). Yet when a child who was horribly oppressed by demons was later brought to the disciples for help, their faith was inadequate to deliver him.

Note that the father of the demon-possessed child appeared to have a more spiritual faith than Christ's disciples did. As the father indicated later when Jesus arrived on the scene, in bringing his oppressed son to the disciples, the father in his own thinking was bringing him to the Lord: "Teacher, I brought You my son" (Mark 9:17).

Now the father begged Jesus Himself to help the boy. Jesus responded by telling the father, "All things are possible to him who believes."

In what transpired next, Jesus showed that the father carried in his own heart the faith necessary to accomplish spiritual feats. When the man cried to Jesus, "I believe!" he was laying hold of the Lord. When he added the plea, "Help my unbelief!" he expressed heart-fasting, the relinquishing of his hold on all human help.

So it was that the instrument of blessing to this family was not the disciples, but the father of the child, because he embraced the Lord and let go of all human help.

Later the disciples came to their Master in confusion and embarrassment, asking why they had failed so miserably. Jesus pointed at once to the smallness of their faith. Then He penetrated to the heart of the problem: "This kind cannot come out by anything but prayer and fasting" (Matthew 17:21, Mark 9:29). He was commending the faith that is attached to the Lord and detached from the world.

My friend in Christ, this is the faith that pleases the Lord and accomplishes His work. Many fast as a means to strong-arm the Lord into releasing a blessing, but God is not impressed if we deny ourselves a week of meals. That is not the ordinance He seeks; He looks for the heart firmly attached to Him that refuses to hold on to the world.

May God place us both on the front lines where prayer and fasting are necessary to do His spiritual work. May He deliver us from a faith that excites the flesh but cannot serve those who are most spiritually oppressed.

Lay hold and let go, my friend. When He returns, may He find us praying and fasting.

Yours, in seeking His life . . .

50 | *True Childlikeness for True Revival*

Dear Humble Heart,

You asked what evidence I believe would demonstrate that the Lord was blessing our country by bringing true revival. My answer is this: an increase in childlikeness.

Many look for more dramatic manifestations—miraculous deliverances, national repentance, masses turning to the Lord, a hunger for holiness, a profound interest in evangelism. All these, to be sure, will blossom as the fruit of revival from God. However, I believe childlikeness is the touchstone of every revival. From the spring of this heart-attitude will bubble all the graces of living character.

But what is this childlikeness?

When Christ spoke of childlikeness, He wasn't referring to the simplicity of a child's beliefs. If that were the case, there would have been no need for the warning the Holy Spirit gave to the Ephesian Christians:

We are no longer to be children, tossed here and there by waves, and carried about by every wind of doctrine, by the trickery of men, by craftiness in deceitful scheming. (Ephesians 4:14)

Children are unable to discern error from the truth; they often choke on the bones while eating the fish. Children believe, without objective evidence, almost anything they hear (especially if they trust the messenger). They do not have the wisdom to discriminate. Jesus never intended His disciples to believe in this manner.

Neither did He intend that we behave as naturally and unpretentiously as children do. Children are free and intuitive and often express their immaturity with unembarrassed ease. But our Lord's call to childlikeness was not a call to immaturity.

Brethren, do not be children in your thinking; yet in evil be babes, but in your thinking be mature. (1 Corinthians 14:20)

A child often gets into trouble because he makes unwise decisions. Children are inexperienced and naive and are not motivated by prudence.

For everyone who partakes only of milk is not accustomed to the word of righteousness, for he is a babe. But solid food is for the mature, who because of practice have their senses trained to discern good and evil. (Hebrews 5:13–14)

When Christ spoke of childlikeness, He was referring to the character of a child—to a person's nature, not his behavior. As I understand it, childlikeness is helpless dependence. The Greek word used to describe the children Jesus welcomed into His arms can be translated "infant of days" (Matthew 18:3). Jesus had in mind the total reliance of a newborn infant. "Of such," said Jesus, "is the kingdom of heaven." Such helplessness refers to who we are, not what we do.

Helpless babes cannot trust their own knowledge, faith, sincerity, strength, efforts, or resources. They must trust another for all things. In the same way, the Lord longs that we trust His adequacy for everything.

Our helpless dependence on the Lord is the clearest evidence of His reviving work in our lives.

The church has grown dangerously sophisticated. We need a revival that makes us childlike rather than childish. Oh, for a sweeping move of the Lord on His people that would result in genuine childlikeness!

Let's pray for one another, that like newborn babes we would desire the sincere milk of the Word, that we may grow.

Bound hand and foot to Jesus . . .

51 | *Your Dependence on Others*

Dear Child of His Providence,

I realize you're uncomfortable with your present circumstances. But God's wise love has placed you there, and we know by faith that what God arranges is best for all.

For a season the Lord has made you dependent on two families. Do not refuse them the opportunity of ministering to you. Your present needs may drain their resources, but this is part of God's high purpose and can become an occasion of blessing for them and for you. In your natural family, God will use your experience redemptively in their lives. Caring for you may be what will bring them to the Savior. Meanwhile all those in your spiritual family will grow as they gladden the heart of God, for Christian love demands that we be concerned for others, willing to deny ourselves so that another may prosper.

Part of dependence on the Lord is dependence on those He chooses as His instruments of provision. It must be a sign of our fallen humanity that blood still comes to our cheeks when we're called on to burden others. Children are willing to depend on their parents, but how parents recoil at the thought of depending on their children!

Elijah was once in a situation like the one you face. It must have been difficult and distasteful for this proud prophet to place himself in the care of the widow of Zarephath, who already was struggling to provide for her only son during a famine. It's thrilling to read in 1 Kings 17 how God empowered Elijah to do what he was told. Because Elijah obeyed by faith, the Lord fulfilled His redemptive purposes and revealed Himself as the God who is more than enough. Elijah did not drain the widow's resources at all; instead he became God's instrument of blessing.

My friend, be content in Jesus, and do not squirm at the providence of God. When we are helplessly dependent on Him, we often are cast on the care of people who love us. Our Lord God could turn stone to bread and provide for you, but most likely that is not His will.

I pray that your burden becomes a blessing, that you give by receiving, and that you display your dependence on the Lord by depending on others.

Yours, in His care . . .

52 | *Leaning on the Lord Is Better Than Clinging*

Dear Trusting Saint,

I was so happy to hear that God has begun to answer my prayer for you and you're now clinging to the Lord in your trial. I've asked the Lord to instruct you how to advance from clinging to leaning on Him, for leaning is better than clinging.

Let me illustrate from the wonderful Song of Solomon. In the early chapters of the book, Solomon describes young love. The Shulammite sought an intimate relationship with her bridegroom lover. She made many of the innocent blunders of young love, and by doing so was hindering the relationship she strove to establish. She was clinging to her lover. "When I found him whom my soul loves, I held on to him and would not let him go" (3:4).

There is a clinging that represents total trust in the Lord, and in this sense we're always to cling to Jesus. We're to hold Him firmly as one holds fast to a life-saving refuge. Clinging to Jesus is the essence of faith. But the clinging in Song of Solomon is different.

This is early love, and the bride in this story was filled with uncertainties and insecurities. She did not cling to the groom as her refuge, but because she feared that if she released her grip he would flee. She was clinging so she would not lose her lover. By clinging, the bride was attempting to secure the relationship by restraint.

She had much to learn of the groom's heart!

A more wonderful scene appears at the close of the book. We see the bride and groom walking together, but this time she isn't frantically clinging to him for fear of losing him. Instead she is "leaning on her beloved" (8:5). Now she doesn't entertain the slightest doubt that the groom will attempt an escape. She has learned that he is not anxious to leave her. He loves her and has no desire to depart. He is content in her presence. This bride had advanced from clinging to leaning. She learned to rest in his love.

My dear friend, I encourage you to relax and lean upon the Lord. Your relationship with Him in no way depends on the strength of your own grip. He doesn't want you to cling to Him as a drowning sailor, but to lean on Him as a confident lover.

Cling if you must—but lean you may! He has vowed He will never leave you.

It was the bride's leaning on her beloved that caused others to marvel and inquire about their relationship: "Who is this coming up from the wilderness, leaning on her beloved?" (8:5). May this also be your witness—a lover at peace with the Bridegroom-Lover.

Please let me know as well how He answers my prayer.

In union with Jesus . . .

53 | *Hold Fast to Helplessness*

Dear Servant of the Lord,

While studying the early chapters of Revelation, I was moved to pray for you in the context of the Holy Spirit's message to the church of Philadelphia. Like Philadelphia, your influence stands out. Your humble spirit and helpless dependence on the Lord have ministered to me.

As I prayed for you, the words of exhortation given to the church of Philadelphia burned into my heart: "Hold fast what you have!" The Holy Spirit spoke those words to the church in Philadelphia in a special way. The saints there were tempted to let go of something they possessed. What was it? The Holy Spirit tells them: "Behold, I have put before you an open door which no one can shut, because *you have a little power*" (3:8).

They possessed little power—they had weakness, helplessness.

They had the blessing of weakness. They were inadequate in themselves. How wonderful to stand before Almighty God without any power of our own. That is where we must ever be, calling on the all-sufficiency of Jesus.

Why should we fear small numbers, little talent, limited resources, lack of ingenuity, or any other weakness? These are not disadvantages in the eyes of the Lord.

Because of the Lord's positive words to the Philadelphia Christians (compared to the reproof and correction He gives to most of the churches in Revelation 2–3), many commentators refer to them as "non-problem believers." But non-problem Christians are often tempted most to let go of helplessness. Any door opened in any way other than by dependence on Jesus will bring only disaster. Do not listen to voices that invite us to become "relevant" to this generation by letting go of our helplessness.

I pray you'll hold fast to what you have. I do not know if you're being tempted to become worldly wise, brave, strong, sufficient, or influential in order to create opportunities, but I have entreated your Keeper to deliver you.

Many doors were open to the Philadelphians as they depended on the Lord. And they were promised that if they remained dependent on Him they would become pillars in the temple of God.

May the grace of God strengthen us both, and may He increase our grip on helplessness.

Yours, in His strength . . .

54 | *Spoon-Feeding*

Dear Instrument of the Lord,

Congratulations on your new ministry position. I pray God will grant you much fruit. I have no advice beyond the words Jesus spoke in John 21 to Peter: "Spoon-feed My sheep" (so is the nuance in the original). By His grace we must be prepared and equipped to spoon-feed His sheep.

Never despise spoon-feeding. We must reject the idea that meat is profound truth and milk is simple truth. Our proud hearts would love to believe that, and then pursue profound truth to dazzle the hungry with our amazing (but indigestible) meat.

Truth is a person—the Lord Jesus. Our message is the person of the Lord Jesus Christ, and we must present Him in the simplest way.

Milk and meat differ only in application. Milk is simple truth unapplied; meat is simple truth applied. Whether truth is meat or milk depends not on the messenger but on the receiver of the message.

Spoon-feed His sheep! That is our high vocation.

Just so, my co-laborer in the gospel, we must not recoil at being spoon-fed ourselves. We too must humbly receive our nourishment from the Lord's people. Yes, all the treasures of wisdom and knowledge are hidden in the Lord Jesus; and, yes, to those who ask He gives bountifully and without upbraiding. We must trust the Holy Spirit to feed us with the substantial Bread of heaven. But that doesn't mean we cannot be spoon-fed.

Spoon-feeding is not unspiritual; it is a part of childlikeness. It may seem spiritual to appear in public and profess that your message comes only from "me, my Bible, and the Holy Spirit!" But this may be nothing but pride. I do not doubt the good Lord may speak directly to our hearts, but it will always be an exception. We need divine help *and* human help. We are a needy people.

God wants to spoon-feed us that we may spoon-feed others. Let us thank Him for the wonderful spoon-feeders He already has sent our way.

May your high calling bless His heart.

His thankful servant . . .

55 | *Don't Dig Where God Isn't Digging*

Dear Fellow Laborer in Christ,

The apostle Paul asked the Corinthians, "Who is led into sin without my intense concern?" I've observed your intense concern for your children in the faith. If sin so breaks the servant's heart, how much more must it wound the heart of the Master! In this concern you are like Jesus.

Your uncompromising position on 1 Thessalonians 5:22— "abstain from every form of evil"— is well-known. You have insisted that the behavior of any Christian be no cause for stumbling. We are to forsake every form of evil that we might be a sterling testimony and witness to the world.

Yet I would ask you to examine 1 Thessalonians 5:22 in the light of the balance of that truth illustrated by 2 Kings 5.

Naaman, the Syrian army commander, had come to saving

faith under the ministry of the prophet Elisha. Now he was distressed about his new life in the place of his employment, where the worship of false gods was obligatory. He went to Elisha and said,

> *When my master goes into the house of Rimmon to worship there, and he leans on my hand and I bow myself in the house of Rimmon, when I bow myself in the house of Rimmon, the LORD pardon your servant in this matter.*

We might expect the prophet to advise him to take a rugged stand for the truth at any cost. As a trophy of God's mercy, surely Naaman must not give the appearance of idol worship; he must refuse to bow down to false Rimmon.

But how did Elisha counsel Naaman? He said, "Go in peace." He did not even warn him of the dangers of compromise.

Elisha was neither condemning nor condoning Naaman's intentions. I believe the prophet was recognizing God's prerogative to deal personally with the testimony of Naaman. Elisha knew the Lord would bring an irresistible conviction to this newborn child of God, and then with a martyr's faith Naaman would take his public stand.

There is a time to say, "Take a rugged stand for the Lord." There is also a time to say, "Go in peace."

God Himself will minister in the lives of those He saves. When He comes, He comes to save His people from their sins. Often the seed grows secretly while His servants sleep, and the Lord Himself gives the increase.

By and by, God in His faithfulness will separate the light from the darkness. He will call the light day and the darkness He will call night.

Therefore we must not dig where God isn't digging; we must not give grief when He does not.

It is sound wisdom to wait for the rising tide to lift the vessel from the sandbank, lest by tugging we cause needless damage.

Encourage every saint to walk in the light of the revelation of Christ; we must be patient until they respond to His light.

Others may call you weak when you tell a young believer to "go in peace," but the bud will eventually open by the power of life if we have not helped it too much with our clumsy but well-meaning hands.

I'm thankful for the Elishas in my life, those who allowed God to deal personally with me and who sent me away in peace.

May the Lord use these words to sweeten your already beautiful life.

Yours, for a holy testimony . . .

56 | *God Is Your River*

Dear Servant of the Living God,

I've received the soul-refreshing news that the Lord is using your life and ministry in public blessing. It is a time for cautious rejoicing, for the tempter has set many snares along the banks of blessing.

The vision in Ezekiel 47 of the temple and its life-giving river is full of instruction for the humble servant of God.

Grace reminds us that the Lord Himself is the River of Life. He is not only the source of the flow, He is the very River! You, as His temple, are only the instrument from which He has chosen to flow.

In the early stages of God's flow through your life, you yourself will be much in view. Like the prophet you will be visibly standing in the stream. As the current strengthens and the water rises, what once trickled at your ankles as a refreshing stream will overwhelm you completely—unless God graces you to get out of the river and watch from the shore. It is from the riverbank that you will best observe the work the Lord is doing through you. In the river you'll be occupied only with survival and will miss God's heart and ministry.

The river cuts its own channel and chooses its own direction. From the shore you will see the end of all the fleshly zeal that spends itself in empty externals and nonessentials. There must be no programs or plans of human origin. No human wisdom can dictate or anticipate the channel the river will carve in its life-giving rush. God makes foolish our dikes and dams as He rescues us from the blessings that flow from our own lives.

Always remember: We are the temple, not the river.

I have every confidence you're standing safely on the shore observing the mystery of God's blessing. This is God's renown, His reputation on the earth. My heart is filled with joy as I think of the harvest that will be His because of your cooperation with His Spirit.

The parched lands, the thirsty deserts, and the Dead Sea, all thank you for allowing Him to use you. I am praying for you.

Rest happy!

Ever your friend, in union with Jesus . . .

57 | *No Strange Fire*

Dear Fellow Pilgrim,

I don't know what you had in mind when you asked me to pray that you might be on fire for the Lord, but I'll tell you how I've been praying. I've asked the Lord to completely deliver you from "strange fire" in your walk and ministry.

The Bible uses the expression "strange fire" to describe a stranger to the Lord.

Nadab and Abihu, the renegade sons of Aaron, offered "strange fire" to the Lord (Leviticus 10). When God refused to send His supernatural fire to consume their sacrifice, they ignited their own flames. They attempted to gain acceptance with God by a fire of their own making. God rejected their fire and judged them for trying to do His work in their own strength.

By contrast, Elijah on Mount Carmel refused to offer the Lord "strange fire," and commanded that the altar and the sacrifice be drenched with water (1 Kings 18). This honored the Lord. Nothing is impossible for the Lord, and He demonstrated His mighty power to confirm the prophet's faith:

> *Then the fire of the LORD fell, and consumed the burnt offering and the wood and the stones and the dust, and licked up the water that was in the trench.*

"Strange fire" is an abomination to the Lord; it is a covenant of works. If our ministry cannot endure the water test now, how will it survive the day when it will be tested by fire?

May God deliver us both from "strange fire." Better far to have no fire at all than a fire of our own making.

I pray you won't be afraid to water down the sacrifice and call down God's fire from above, and that you'll burn with the fire that is no stranger to Him.

Yours, in the New Covenant . . .

58 | *In Faith, Let Jesus Sleep*

Dear Fellow Believer,

I do not think I can define faith for you, at least not in a way that will satisfy you. The Bible often describes and illustrates faith, but to my knowledge the closest it comes to a definition is in Hebrews 11:1—"Now faith is the assurance of things hoped for, the conviction of things not seen."

But even these words do not offer defining limits to faith. *Faith*, like many Bible words *(fear, mercy, glory, love)*, is too great to be confined to a definition.

I once reduced faith to three basic principles:

1. Come to the end of human resources.

2. Appeal to the Lord Jesus as the only One in whom help is found.

3. Stand aside and behold the Lord doing the work that only God can do.

That sounded very spiritual to me—and all-inclusive—until I studied the passage about how Jesus slept in the boat on the stormy sea.

When the disciples were unable to manage the ship and began to fear for their lives, it appeared that they (1) had exhausted their human resources; when they awakened Jesus and cried out for His salvation, they (2) appealed to Him as the only One who could rescue them; when they saw Jesus still the storm and calm the sea, they (3) witnessed God's sovereign power.

Did Jesus congratulate them for a healthy faith? Was it their faith that caused them to cry out to Him for help? No, for Mark tells us that Jesus asked them, "How is it that you have *no faith?*" (4:40).

Why did they fear they would sink to the bottom of the lake? Was Jesus less in control when asleep? No, He only *appeared* detached and unconscious. He was testing their faith. The disciples could have expressed that faith by allowing Jesus to continue to sleep, to rest until they had fulfilled His words, "Let us go over to the other side."

Although I cannot define faith, I fear that much that passes for faith is actually unbelief. Unbelief also cries out for a miracle. Unbelief can even spring God to action; it was unbelief and not faith that caused the Lord Jesus to calm the sea. What a wonderful God we have, to be so patient with unbelief that He responds to it with His mightiest displays of power!

In our weakness and desperation, all of us will wake up the

Lord Jesus at one time or another. When we do, He will not be angry. He will mildly rebuke us as He did the disciples so long ago, "Why are you so timid? How is it that you have no faith?" But then He will rise and do a great work to lift our spirits and revive us yet again. He responds to unbelief in order to encourage faith.

Faith can be content when God doesn't stir—when Jesus is sleeping. Faith is letting Jesus sleep. Unbelief panics when Jesus sleeps.

Faith is a living thing. The most important thing about faith is Jesus, the Object of our faith.

Let us both take our eyes off faith and fix them on Jesus. Asleep or awake, He will guide our ship safely through the storm.

His trusting child . . .

59 | *Hamstring Those Worldly Horses*

Dear Servant of the Lord,

I was excited to hear how God has lifted you to a place of wide and meaningful influence. I pray the Lord will make your feet like hinds' feet in those high places, where your safety comes not from vigilance to be surefooted but from His ability to keep you humble on the dizzy heights.

As I sought the Lord for the most practical way to intercede for you, I was reminded of the word God gave to Joshua when Israel battled for northern Palestine. God told him to "hamstring their horses and burn their chariots with fire" (Joshua 11:6).

What an odd and illogical command! By destroying such horsepower and attack transport, wouldn't Israel be casting away a tremendous opportunity to build up their own arsenal? Wouldn't it make more sense to use the enemy's equipment for the Lord?

Israel had to learn, as we must, that the weapons of our warfare are not carnal but divinely powerful for the destruction of fortresses set up against the knowledge of God. It pleases the Lord when we're willing to put away the wisdom and methods of this world to trust Him alone.

You're now on the front lines of the conflict. Many will be powerfully influenced by your actions. I'm praying that you'll not fear to hamstring the methods of this world. God has placed you on a high hill where worldly chariots will be of no use. Any horse or chariot that offers victory apart from Him must be lamed and burned.

If you follow this course, I'm certain you'll be misunderstood. You'll be told to use the world's weapons for His glory, as instruments of His blessing. You'll be considered foolish for operating on heavenly principles. The shallow and jealous will prophesy against you; many will wag their heads and accuse you of fanaticism.

May God keep you as His chosen instrument for good in the high seat. As always your victory will be from the Lord alone; as always your provision will be from the Lord alone; as always your usefulness will be from the Lord alone.

Some boast in chariots, and some in horses; but we will boast in the name of the LORD, our God. (Psalm 20:7)

I love you, dear friend, and I will ever ask the Lord to make your feet beautiful upon the mountains to proclaim the good news.

We will watch the Lord fight for you.

Yours, in His cause . . .

60 | *Obey the Lord's Heart*

Dear Faithful Servant of the Lord,

I know you're disappointed that so many have taken a stand against your proposed ministry. There is safety in a multitude of counselors, but not infallibility.

I won't offer any opinion on the ministry itself, but with joy I remind you that your service is ultimately to the Lord Jesus. It is His heart you must please. Before Him you stand, and to Him you will render a final account.

The opposition from the brothers there appears to spring from their deep love for you and their concern that you may be straying from the path of obedience.

One kind of obedience is content to conform to the letter; a deeper obedience issues from the heart. Sometimes heart-obedience can even appear like disobedience.

The account in Luke 17 of the ten lepers might apply to your situation. When the ten men cried out to the Lord for mercy, He gave them this command: "Go, show yourselves to the priests."

It was a simple command, easy to understand and do. The lepers were required only to appear before the priests to receive the test for leprosy, according to the laws prescribed in the book of Leviticus.

As they were on their way to obey this simple command, a great change swept over their bodies. The power of God came upon them and they all were instantaneously healed.

Now what should they do? Nine of the former lepers apparently did nothing more than fulfill the letter of the command. But the other man (a Samaritan) turned back, praising God with a voice heard around the countryside. When he saw his Healer, he fell on his face and worshiped Him. Jesus did not rebuke him—"I sent you to the priests! Why are you here?" No, Jesus said to him, "Were there not ten cleansed? But the nine—where are they?" It is clear the Lord Jesus expected all ten lepers to return. He intended each of them to go beyond simply obeying the letter of His command and to respond with the deeper obedience of the heart.

To eyes of flesh the nine appear to be obedient servants. But only the Samaritan who returned to praise God obeyed with New Covenant obedience.

I know that you obey from the heart and are sometimes misunderstood. Some may even accuse you of leaving the path of obedience to act independently in your union with Jesus. Few will have the insight to understand there is a deeper obedience that goes so far beyond the letter of the law. If you're in such a situation, do not criticize those who condemn you. Only worship Jesus and minister to His heart.

When the Lord Jesus asked, "Where are the nine?" the Samaritan wisely offered no answer. You must be silent and know that the Lord is pleased with you. Do not try to defend yourself; God is your defense. If you must, leave behind you those who are content with obeying the letter only. But follow your heart to the Savior's feet.

I'm not suggesting that you disregard the counsel offered to you, but I encourage you to do whatever you know would minister to the heart of the Lord Jesus, even if you must return to His feet alone. God desires the heart a million times more than mere letter-obedience.

The laws of relationship with Jesus will keep you safe. By all means obey the Lord—but may God grace you to obey in spirit and not in the letter only. He will vindicate your ministry by and by. Be patient!

Your friend in the grace of God . . .

61 | *The Secret of Victory*

My Dear Friend in Christ,

My only purpose for this note is the desire to share the light God poured into my soul in my recent meditation on Exodus 17:8–16. I needed to be refreshed in the truths of God's victory in the Lord Jesus, and there's much to learn about this here in the valley of Rephidim.

The Amalekites, by cowardly attacks on the fainthearted, the weary, and the slow of foot (Deuteronomy 25:17–19), had exasperated and harassed God's redeemed people. (The straggler is always the most vulnerable, the most likely to be ambushed. This thought convicted me to keep better pace with the body of Christ. Safety as well as edification is to be found in the church.)

Now, at the approach of the army of Amalek for formal battle, Moses instructed Joshua, "Choose men for us, and go out, fight against Amalek." Moses also added, "I will station myself on the top of the hill with the staff of God in my hand."

No doubt Joshua selected the best available soldiers, the most courageous, skillful, and disciplined men he could muster. But the victory did not depend upon the army. Victory was God's gift to them. While Moses pointed the dead stick (that's what the staff was) toward God and heaven, Israel's struggling soldiers in the valley enjoyed victory. When Moses' hands grew heavy and began to fall, the tide turned and the redeemed of the Lord began to suffer defeat, until Aaron and Hur stationed themselves at Moses' side to steady his arms. Every moment of that day's conflict was determined by what took place on the mountain.

Victory is a relationship with the Lord Jesus Christ and is accomplished through union with Him. The staff pointing toward God and heaven symbolized man and the direction of his heart.

The army of Amalek was the first to confront Israel after the Red Sea crossing. It isn't surprising that the Lord would teach His people so early in their nationhood that *relationship with Him* is victory. Victory is a gift to be received and not a reward of conflict.

It's one thing to fight when victory is assured, but how frustrating to engage in a battle lost before it begins. How many of us fight such losing battles! If we refuse to depend upon the Lord, we've lost before we begin. We cannot avoid clashes with the enemy, but our victory never comes from human strength, human wisdom, human resources. We are victorious only in union with the Lord Himself.

Let me pass on one further thought from this passage, on the unexpected revelation that Moses' hands grew heavy (17:12). I would have expected to read, "Joshua's hands grew heavy," for surely Joshua's sword weighed more than Moses' staff, and we would think the conflict in the valley was more exhausting than the ministry on the mountain. But the staff represented the spiritual battle, and the mountain the place of victory. Spiritual things will bring our greatest weariness. In trusting God we faint, in prayer we become distracted, in worship we become formal, in truly meeting the Lord in the Bible we become exhausted. It is far more draining to meet God in reality than to fight Amalek in the valley. Our hands become heavy in the prayer closet, at the altar, at the Lord's Table, in the Book, and in the assembly. Yet we must prevail with the Lord in order to prevail over Amalek.

I know you believe these things, but I needed to be quickened to them again. We cannot be reminded enough that in ourselves we are but dead sticks. Our only hope is to point toward God and heaven.

You've often been to me as Aaron and Hur were to Moses—a helper of my helplessness. Times without number, you have propped me up in the direction of Jesus. Thank you, my friend.

Rejoicing in His victory . . .

62 | *Honoring the Lord with Your Questions*

Dear Lover of Truth,

Did you overstate the truth when you said, "I'll never question God about anything"? I have no doubt you intended to express the folly of clay disputing with the Potter. But I hope you've left a door open to the wonderful opportunities for knowing God that often come through questions.

God loves questions. But not all questions are alike. Some expose childlikeness and are rooted in faith, while others are grounded in doubt and reveal the pride of the natural heart. Our questions can appear identical on the outside, but God, who discerns the heart, knows which questions honor Him and which do not.

Zacharias, father of John the baptizer, and Mary, mother of the Lord Jesus, each received a special revelation from heaven through the angel Gabriel. In both cases the angel announced tidings of great joy. The aged priest Zacharias learned that God had opened his wife's barren womb and that in her old age she would bear him a son. Mary of Nazareth learned that by the power of the Holy Spirit she would conceive a baby in her virgin womb.

Both Zacharias and Mary were told impossible things. Zacharias and Elizabeth would need a miracle to conceive a child in their old age; Mary would need a miracle to conceive a Son in her virgin body.

Both Zacharias and Mary heard the word of Gabriel in fear. And both asked a question.

Zacharias asked, "How shall I know this for certain? For I am an old man, and my wife is advanced in years."

Mary asked, "How can this be, since I am a virgin?"

Both sought to understand how God would accomplish such a promised wonder. Yet Zacharias was struck dumb for his unbelieving question, while Mary's question has been immortalized as an illustration of childlike faith.

Many saints have gone forward with the Lord because they asked questions *from hearts that believed God.* One may ask God *how* He will accomplish the impossible with feeble means, but we must never ask Him if He *can* or *will* keep His promise. If God has spoken, He will do what He has said, whatever obstacles may lie in the way.

Zacharias desired evidence, not information. Mary never doubted that God would perform what He had spoken; she wondered only by what means He would perform it.

I know some who in the name of faith encourage Christians to crucify all questions. But it isn't wrong to ask questions in faith.

There may be countless questions that do not dishonor the Lord or impugn His character.

On the other hand, we should never ask unbelieving questions. Unbelief will never honor Him. Be forever on guard against unbelief in all its subtle forms. May God strike us dumb, as He did Zacharias, until we open our mouths in believing praise to Him.

But faith that struggles to believe is still faith and as such pleases God. Unbelief differs from struggling faith in that unbelief has no *will* to believe God.

Some questions keep the weaned child from resting against the mother; those we must flee. Other questions press us to His bosom; let us not be afraid to vent them.

Let us know God by all means. And let us honor Him with faith-building questions.

Yours, in the heart-knowledge of the Lord . . .

63 | *Don't Be Troubled When the Lord Isn't*

Dear Saint of the Most High God,

I sensed a troubled spirit in your last letter to me. It appeared that the possibilities of evil still lurking in your heart had made you question whether you're making any spiritual progress at all.

All living things grow, and I know you are growing! Don't be impatient to reach maturity in the Lord Jesus.

I offer you the Lord's comfort from His beautiful words to Peter and the disciples with him: "Let not your heart be troubled; believe in God, believe also in Me."

The Lord had just revealed to the apostle (at the end of John 13) the folly of his empty boasts of loyalty and the weakness of his flesh to remain faithful through even a single night: "Truly, truly, I say to you, a cock shall not crow, until you deny Me three times."

Could such words be true? Instead of Peter being faithful to the Lord Jesus by laying down his life, would the morning light reveal a three-time traitor? Could Peter have been that blind to his true spiritual condition?

No wonder Peter's heart was troubled.

If Jesus made the same disclosure to our hearts, wouldn't we respond with a flood of fear and trembling? It's a scary thing when Christ reveals to our hearts the wide gulf that stands between our desire to serve Him and the reality of our weakness. When we see our hearts as He sees them, we're compelled to cry out, "Have patience with me, O Lord! I've seen my heart! I fear I shall never be truly loyal!" It's no surprise that we're troubled when we suddenly discover our true condition.

At such a time and to such a spiritual state, Jesus speaks the comforting words, "Let not your heart be troubled; believe in God, believe also in Me."

What? Let not my heart be troubled? When the light has revealed that my love is self, loyalty is wind, dedication is denial, and endurance is fleeting? My heart is filled with trouble. Where is the comfort?

Here is the comfort: It's as if Jesus said to Peter, "Peter, I know you and I love you. I know your weakness, your inadequacy, your immaturity. I have seen the worst in you, Peter, and *I am not troubled by it!*

"In spite of the worst in you, I will realize your highest aspirations. You are astounded, shocked, overwhelmed, humbled at the discovery of where you are in your spiritual development. But I am not dismayed by what I observe. You will eventually be fully conformed to Me.

"There is a process, Peter. You will learn so much about Me, about yourself, about our union. And I have perfect peace about your ultimate maturity. You *will* follow Me. Have faith! Believe in God! Believe in Me! The very worst in you will never stand in the way of My highest purposes for your life.

"Therefore, Peter, let not your heart be troubled."

We are together in our desire to manifest Christ in our transformed characters. We must never be troubled by that which doesn't trouble Him. He suffers not a moment of anxiety about our immaturity. We can be as free from care about our own perseverance and conformity to Christ as He is.

I've written this letter to refresh your spirit with the good news that only unbelief can hinder your maturity in Christ. The worst in you is no hindrance.

May Christ be our Patience as we go forward—untroubled—in Him!

Slowly developing in Christ . . .

64 | *Your Joy for the Bride and Groom*

Dear Servant of the Lord,

The sadness you expressed about dwindling attendance at your home Bible studies may arise from a misreading of the hearts of your well-fed flock. Losing disciples can be an occasion for gladness rather than sadness, for you may be losing them to Jesus.

John the baptizer's experience may well be your own. The uninstructed thought they were bringing him bad news when they told of the growing success of Jesus' ministry at the expense of John's (John 3:26). But John understood the ways of God and his heart leapt. John explained that he was not the Groom but the friend of the Groom. The Lord Jesus had all claims on the bride. The friend of the Groom experienced fullness of joy when he saw the bride and Groom united.

"He must increase," John said, "but I must decrease."

It is no loss when men stop depending on one another and begin to cling to the Lord. To be sure, there's a correct way to flock around the servants of the Lord. But even that is beset with many snares. How fast creature streams run dry; how quickly human resources are depleted. Man is a frail staff on which to lean.

How wonderfully simple is the truth, "He who has the bride is the Bridegroom."

We should be sad when we do not see the bride coming to the Groom. But to see the bride delighting to be in union with her Groom is ever our joy and satisfaction. What rivers of blessedness it should be for us to hear the news, "You are losing disciples to Jesus." May He increase; may we decrease.

I rejoice in your labor, for I'm sure you never desired to attract the Lord's bride to yourself.

Press on, my friend in the gospel, press on! Let us both be the Groom's faithful friends and promote His exclusive relationship with the bride. Let us honor Him by keeping our hands off His bride.

Rejoicing in His increase . . .

65 | *Be a Song*

Dear Worshiper of God,

I'll be happy to comment on Ephesians 5:19–20 and attempt to answer your question, "What music is spoken of in this wonderful passage?" How shall we "speak to one another in psalms and hymns and spiritual songs"?

Not all believers are privileged or gifted to carry God's message through the ministry of music. He has undoubtedly raised up anointed artists for that purpose, and through them He powerfully and movingly taps the waters in the deepest springs of the human spirit. But Paul encourages all Christians to engage in this ministry:

> . . . *singing and making melody with your heart to the Lord, always giving thanks for all things in the name of our Lord Jesus Christ to God, even the Father.*

How can this be?

It appears that the encouragement is not to sing to men, but to God. The ministry is not to *sing* a song, but to *be* a song; it is a spiritual ministry of music, not a physical ministry of music.

Notice too that gratitude is the melody in our heart that pleases Him. When we humbly thank the Lord for all things, convinced by faith that He has lovingly and wisely allowed them into our lives to conform us to His image, we have worshiped the Lord in song.

Those around us may not hear the notes of praise we raise to the Lord, but they behold in our expressions the music of heaven. By silently singing our melody of praise to God, others behold our joy and we have ministered in psalms, hymns, and spiritual songs.

The thankful believer is a delight to be around. His whole life is a sweet psalm. The silent heart-song rises to the Lord as incense from an altar. It needs no vocal cords or words. It is an ineffable, soundless melody bursting forth with thanksgiving, worship, and praise to God. Every Christian can make melody in his heart to the Lord, even without a tongue.

The saint who walks in the Spirit and lives in gratitude is ministering unto the world through psalms, hymns, and spiritual songs—though not an audible word is spoken. This is the ministry of music Paul referred to in Ephesians 5.

So let us speak to one another by our inner music to the Lord. When King David wrote of the new song that God put in the heart, he said, "Many will see and fear and will trust in the Lord."

The song in the heart can be seen, not heard. The Lord hears it; man sees it. May God enable us, by our silent gratitude to Him, to speak the music of heaven to the sons of men.

This world sadly needs a song. So sing!

Rejoicing at all times . . .

66 | *Only God Brings Growth, Only God's Work Lasts*

Dear Fellow Laborer in the Lord,

May I answer in love your recent thoughts on "wood, hay, and stubble"?

Your warning that all of our works will be tested by fire was powerful and well-spoken. Who would quarrel with the proposition you so ably developed, that all the works of the flesh shall be burned up? Beyond all reasonable doubt, only that which the Holy Spirit accomplishes through our lives will remain; those things we have done in our own energy will be consumed.

My question is this: Are you wise to assume from the context of 1 Corinthians 3 that the expression *wood, hay, and stubble* refers to the works generated by our own flesh? It seems to me as if God chose that figure to illustrate an altogether different truth.

Paul in this passage was addressing the problem of sectarianism, and the "jealousy and strife" (3:3) that go with it. The Corinthian believers had split up their fellowship into at least four distinctive groups. One group identified with Paul, another with Peter, another with Apollos, and a fourth attempted to make Christ Himself the head of a clique. The Holy Spirit used two illustrations—the first agricultural, the second architectural—to show the unity of all Christian workers and the glory of God as the One who causes growth.

Both illustrations demonstrated an identical truth: Man is only the instrument; the Lord accomplishes the work.

In the agricultural illustration, the Holy Spirit points out that some plant, others water, but it is God who brings growth. It would be wrong to exalt the one who plowed above the one who planted, or the one who planted above the one who watered. All are God's instruments, working together with the Lord. It is God who performs the work that guarantees the harvest.

Likewise, in the architectural illustration there are a variety of workers. Each combines his skill toward the accomplishment of the whole. One may lay a foundation, another may build upon it. Those who build upon it may do so in various ways. In building, some are required to do rugged work, while others do more delicate work. Some work with large tools, others with precision instruments, but all work together to build the same building.

The Holy Spirit drew this illustration from a culture that used gold, silver, precious stones, wood, hay, and stubble in building. Some did fancy work with gold and silver and precious stones. Others did basic framing with wood, while others worked on the thatched roofs with hay and stubble. In God's estimation, the work of wood, hay, and stubble was as honorable as the work with gold, silver, and precious stones. As in farming, where the one who plants has no more glory than the one who waters, so in construction the one who finishes the cosmetic touches has no more glory than the one who digs the foundation or lays on the roof.

The illustration of wood, hay, and stubble seems to be a warning against sectarianism. We are all one body, and we are each to work with our gifts—however humble they might be—while trusting in the Lord.

We will all be tested by fire. The ministry of planting will be tested by fire, and so will the ministry of watering; the ministry of foundation laying will be tested by fire, and so will the ministry of building a superstructure. God will test those who build with gold, silver, precious stones, wood, hay, and stubble. Some gold, silver, and precious stones may not survive the fire test; some wood, hay, and stubble will survive.

So we must not live by the works of the flesh, nor must we attach ourselves to men and ministries in an unhealthy way.

There's only a shade of difference in our doctrinal views, and not even a shade of difference in our direction. I share with you a cordial agreement in all the essentials of the gospel of God's grace.

I'm sure the Lord will wonderfully bless your teaching, because it is He who gives the increase.

I pray that our differences will never go beyond the illustrations we choose.

Yours, in the cause of Christ . . .

67 | *Christian Writing Must Be Christ-Centered*

Dear Messenger of the Lord,

I've joyfully heard of the door of opportunity opened to you with the publication of your writings. No doubt you'll emerge into public life—and into the personal dangers which accompany success. Solomon exclaimed, "A word fitly spoken, how good it is!" The same word fitly written should be even better, for the lifespan of a written word far exceeds the short season of the same word spoken.

You don't need to be reminded that all honors are seductive and dangerous, that worldly greatness is unsatisfying and vain, and that human approval is fleeting and momentary. They are the snares that accompany publication.

I will pray for you Psalm 126:4—"Restore our captivity, O LORD, as the streams in the South."

In the summer, streambeds in southern Canaan are perfectly

dry. In the winter God restores these watercourses and supplies an abundance of water.

Many watercourses exist today—books and authors in abundance—but my friend, the land is parched and the streams are dry. More times than not, what is committed to the printed page is death. The watercourses have dried up under the withering drought of the dissatisfying philosophies of this world's wisdom.

But your writings are life and will bring refreshment from the Lord. The streams in the south will flow again, and like the water that flowed from Ezekiel's temple they will bring luxurious fruit wherever they flow. For this I will earnestly pray.

Allow me to pass on Solomon's wisdom (from near the end of Ecclesiastes) to those called to be authors.

> *The Preacher sought to find delightful words and to write words of truth correctly. The words of wise men are like goads, and masters of these collections are like well-driven nails; they are given by one Shepherd. But beyond this, my son, be warned: the writing of many books is endless, and excessive devotion to books is wearying to the body.*

Should God continue to guide you to print the unsearchable riches of Christ, do follow Solomon's simple counsel. Let me especially point you to three principles.

The first is found in the words, which "are given by one Shepherd." My friend, be certain that what you commit to paper is from the Lord. You must be taught of God. You must guard yourself by His Spirit from printing your own ideas. God's dear people do not advance in the Lord through possibilities or probabilities. They need certainties.

Until the Lord quickens your heart to some revelation of the Lord Jesus Christ, you're not ready to have it printed or published (nor would you desire to). Wait patiently before Him, that your spirit might be fed by one Shepherd. When you have received bread and fish from His hand, then you are ready to pass it on to the hungry. What you write must be given by one Shepherd.

The second principle is suggested by the comparison of a wise man's words to goads and well-driven nails. Take great care that what you write is simple and pointed. Present light that Christians can walk in, not light that dazzles. Do not ramble. Do not be afraid to drive home the truth of God. Put a sharp barb on your application of truth so that all who read it might exercise their wills toward Him.

The truth of God is a nail, His word is a hammer, and your Spirit-controlled expression of God's Word is the authority that will goad the reader to action. If the truth of God isn't burning in your soul, there's little chance that your writing can spur anyone else toward the Lord.

Write if you're so inclined—but let God initiate the writing and anoint it as you proceed.

The final principle concerns something for which we're specifically told to "be warned." And this is the warning: There is no end to the writing of books. But the heart seeking after the knowledge of God is selective. Such a heart discriminates in its reading and has great difficulty finding green pastures and living waters among the writings of men and women. Therefore let your works be always saturated with Christ. Publication is not the end of writing; the goal of the Christian author is to communicate Christ. Do not weary the reader with flowery words which do not lead to Jesus.

Do not weary yourself by long hours of editing material which cannot nourish the hungry spirit. Find acceptable and delightful words with which to convey truth correctly.

May the Shepherd gift you to communicate in print those precious revelations of Jesus which will edify all.

Yours, in the manifestation of Christ . . .

68 | *Fade Away, and Let God Speak Through You*

Dear Fellow Servant of Christ,

Thank you for telling me of your upcoming opportunities to preach and teach, so I may pray intelligently for you. I've been burdened to pray that you won't finish even one message. Let me explain what I mean.

I've been studying the book of Job and especially the young man Elihu, who was so powerfully used by God to turn Job's heart toward the Lord. Unlike Job's other three friends, Elihu turned away from human reasoning and exalted the Lord. Again and again Elihu lifted Job's eyes from the dunghill of human experience to the majesty of the Lord in heaven.

In every discourse in the book of Job we see clearly where one man concluded his speech and another began—but not with Elihu. Suddenly, while Elihu was still bragging on the Lord, we read, "The LORD answered Job out of the whirlwind. . . ." As Elihu held the exalted Lord before the eyes of Job, God began to speak. Job was listening to Elihu and curiously found himself listening to God.

God finished Elihu's message.

My friend, I pray that your ministry might be like that of Elihu. He was a humble man who did not trust his own wisdom. He did not attempt to set Job straight, nor did he condemn the advice that preceded him. Elihu simply presented the Lord. As Elihu spoke, Job found himself in the presence of the Lord Himself. How wonderful when the Lord speaks through the chaos and whirlwind of human reasoning to proclaim Himself!

I desire for myself the same thing I pray for you. I long to fade away when I speak, as Elihu did, in order that God may finish the discourse. I want Him to finish the message.

I pray God will use you as He used Elihu, not to give profound answers to profound questions, but to present the glorious Lord Jesus as the only Object of worship and adoration. As you present Christ, He will speak and carry the listener to reality and repentance. Heaven's work is done when *God* finishes the instruction.

To present the message you so earnestly desire to send forth, prepare your messages well, and make every point Christ-centered and simple; then fade, my friend, fade! Decrease in the glory of His increasing.

May we both fade away in the radiance of the Christ we are privileged to hold before all of God's Jobs.

Your praying friend in Christ . . .

69 | *Hold On to the Rod of God's Grace*

Dear Friend in Christ,

Yes, I've meditated on Moses' sin in striking the rock at Kadesh (Numbers 20). Like many other students of the Word of God I've been awed at God's severity in denying Moses entrance into the Promised Land (although we learn in the Gospels that on the mount of Christ's transfiguration Moses finally did enter the land).

Trying to discover his actual transgression is to attempt to unravel the mystery of iniquity, for each sin is a seed-plot of many offenses. In various places in the Bible the Holy Spirit accused Moses of speaking rashly with his lips, and of impatience, pride, disobedience, irreverence, and unbelief. Yet here a greater offense than these is implied. I believe the judgment of God raged against Moses because he destroyed a most beautiful picture of union with Christ.

God commanded Moses to speak to the rock with the understanding that the rock would release its blessing to satisfy the thirst of the nation. God intended to show that His blessing can be continually enjoyed through intimate communion with the rock. This was God's illustration of pure grace.

The command to "take the rod" must be understood in the light of how Israel's history had unfolded. This was not the rod of judgment by which God plagued the Egyptians and opened the Red Sea. Moses did not take his own rod in his hand, for we read, "Moses took the rod from before the LORD." The only rod kept before the Lord was Aaron's rod—a rod of grace, not judgment. This was the very rod that overnight was laden with buds and blossoms and ripe almonds by the miracle of God (Numbers 17) after 250 leaders of Israel had challenged the authority of Moses and Aaron. The miracle identified the man of God's choosing. It was a dead rod, yet produced fruit by the life of God. As "a sign against the rebels" (17:10), the Lord had commanded that this rod be kept before Him in the Tabernacle with the Ark of the Covenant.

This is the very rod Moses now took in his hand as he stood before the second generation of murmurers. This is the rod with which he smote the rock.

In God's intended picture, Moses was to stand before the God-appointed rock as a priest, a priest with the rod of grace in his hand. He was simply to speak to the rock for blessing to pour forth.

How shocking to instead see this priest smite the rock with the rod of grace! The rod was delicate with white blossoms and buds and almonds; can you imagine what it looked like after being used to beat the rock? By striking the rock, Moses not only ruined the picture of the rock as Christ, but also ruined the precious picture of the rod as God's grace. For this, Moses was severely chastened.

So it is in our day that we have seen grace take such a beating. We have beheld rude libertines attempt to demand blessings from Christ by beating Him over the head with His own covenant. May God deliver us from such.

Your question gave me the opportunity to remind my heart afresh that I am His priest, I hold His beautiful grace in my hand, He has invited me to humbly address the once-smitten Rock, and He has promised me the fullness of blessing that flows through this union.

Aren't you glad that we need only stand before God as His priests, hold firmly in our hand the living rod of grace, and speak to our Lord Jesus Christ to receive the undeserved blessing of God?

Yours, by His grace . . .

70 | *Safe and Sound in His Love*

Dear Friend in Christ,

May the love of God in Christ Jesus support you in your hour of loss and separation.

We both know too much to grieve as those who have no hope. May the fact that you cannot be separated from the love of God sweeten this temporary loss.

In his desire to ground us in the love from which there is no separation, Paul in Romans 8 exhausts every possibility of separation. Famine may separate us from food and water; nakedness may strip away clothing and shelter; peril may sever us from fleshly security; the sword may cut us off from peace; death may detach us from life and from family, home, and friends—but what of it? What can separate us from the love of God which is in Christ Jesus? Nothing!

What does it matter if tribulation separates us from ease, distress from contentment, persecution from fair and just dealings? We are still bound to the Lord Jesus by the love of God.

Since we can never be parted from Him, we should not be discouraged when we suffer a temporal separation. Whatever disconnects us from temporal things can never reach the Lord. What peace we have to know that the wild waves of the enemy cannot dampen the throne of God!

We will always be plagued with separators of some kind, but we never can be separated from God or His love. In all the created universe nothing that can bring about such a breach—not angels or principalities or powers, not the past or the present or the future, not anything from above or beneath or around. No created thing, visible or invisible, can tear us away from the love of God which is in Christ Jesus our Lord.

For a little while we are subject to annoying separators: trouble, misery, ill-treatment, hunger, exposure, dangers, wars, death. But Paul's persuasion is ours as well. We are safe and sound in the love of God.

Meditate on this security, and I know you will conquer through your heavenly Lover, as you endure the separations of this fleeting life. I am praying for you as you lead the fellowship into God's rest.

Yours, in the indissoluble love of God . . .

Scripture Index